My Crown and Glory
It's NOT About The Hair

Six Fundamental Principles to Heal Emotional Wounds

and Build Healthy Self-Esteem

Special Message:

Let your light shine, inside and out!
With Love- For Love,
Sandra Dubose

My Crown and Glory
It's NOT About The Hair

Six Fundamental Principles to Heal Emotional Wounds

and Build Healthy Self-Esteem

SANDRA DUBOSE

The Bald Beauty Queen of Self-Esteem

Published by Createspace

My Crown and Glory
Copyright ©2012 by Sandra Dubose-Gibson

ISBN-13: 978-1478375364

ISBN-10: 1478375361

Edited by: Jessica Martinez

Cover photography and graphic design by
Chris Charles, Creative Silence Photo & Design
www.creativesilencephoto-design.com

This book is dedicated to my daughters,

Miyah Danaye
and
Elajah Michele Gibson

You are my soul's inspiration.
There is no accomplishment in my life that could ever
match the pride I feel of simply being your mother.

I love you both with all my heart.

Contents

Acknowledgements

First and foremost I give thanks to God for all my blessings. Lord you will forever be my source of strength and my song.

To my husband John Gibson: Because of your love and the sacrifices you have made, I am able to pursue my dreams. Thank you for believing in me from day one. I love you for life.

To my oldest daughter Miyah: I see myself in you and yet so much more that I only wish I could be. You are my pride and joy. Thank you for making me laugh and being my Angel.

To my baby girl Elajah: Thank you for your smile and dimples that always make my day. Your hugs and kisses of encourage-ment on my forehead fill my life with joy. I love you so much.

To my mother Gussie Dubose: Thank you for being a suppor-tive and wonderful mother, friend and role model. I love and appreciate you more than words can say.

To my sister Linda Smith: Thank you for being a great big sister and for always having my back. Love to you, Royal and my dar-ling nephew Christopher.

To my brother Rick Mitchell: You are an amazing big brother and friend. Thank you for your unconditional love and support. Love to you, Robin, Christian, Shekinah, and Joshua.

To my Goddaughters, Lelia Fletcher and Imeutinyan Ugiagbe: From the moment we met, you filled my life with sunshine and happy days. You will always have a special place in my heart.

To my In-Laws Johnny and Johnnie Mae McCoy: Thank you for your continued love, support and prayers. Love to you, Jamie, Jabou, Johnnay and the entire Gibson Family.

To my Godparents, Pastor Francina and Elder Leon Corbett: Thank you for always interceding on my behalf with prayer, love and sound advice. Love to you, Tawana, Derrick, and Tara.

To my Best Friends and their families: Reverend Sala Chrispin, Takisha Reid-Holloway, D'wana Brown-White, Dianne Pritchard and Kenneth Taylor. When I think of friends that are more like family, I immediately think of you. I love you BFF's.

To my business mentor and friend Dr. David Washington: Thank you for believing in me, and sharing your knowledge and expertise while leading the way to success by example.

To Elder Anthony O. Vann: Thank you for being a wonderful friend, support team and vessel of God. Love to you and all of the Kings and Queens of the Noire Productions Family.

To Chris Charles: You are an amazing photographer and graphic design artist. It was an absolute pleasure to work with you and I look forward to the next opportunity. www.creativesilencephoto-design.com

Special Thanks to the following: The Link Sister Circle, Paul Banks and Family, The McKenzie Family, The Dubose Family, The Sherman Family, Sheila Belkin, Lisa Thomas, Doreen Rainey, Madaha Kinsey-Lamb, Pretty in Pink Foundation, Clayton Brock, Dr. Emekauwa, WSHA Shaw University Radio, and the Alopecia Community of the Triangle. To my former co-workers at Verizon, the High School for Violin and Dance, Wake Technical Community College and NC State University Poole College of Management especially Sharmeen Williams-Nokes, Anitra Hill, Charles Canteen and Carlos Sanford.

My Crown and Glory
It's NOT About The Hair

Six Fundamental Principles to Heal Emotional Wounds

and Build Healthy Self-Esteem

Introduction

The first real gun I ever saw was the shotgun that was pointed at the head of my beloved high school sweetheart. He was at it again, reenacting the dramatic performance he would give whenever I conjured up just enough sanity and clarity to tell him that I did not think we should be together anymore. Although I loved him, I knew that our relationship was unhealthy because the line where he ended and I began had become a blur to me. Somewhere down on Lovers' Lane I lost a part of my identity and I knew I needed to find it. He could sense that I was searching and it scared him because he was not emotionally or mentally prepared to break those ties.

Time and time again he would threaten to kill himself, all the while convincing me that it would be my fault if he did. "How could you live with yourself knowing that you took my life?" he would ask. "You are my life!" We loved each other more than we loved ourselves. The relationship did not start with abuse; we were great together for a season and shared a genuine connection. Unfortunately, we were two broken halves that depended on one another to feel whole, and that imbalance became an addictive recipe for disaster and self-destruction. After his guilt trip, if I did not abort my mission and apologize for suggesting that we break up, he would turn his anger and violence away from himself and towards me.

I knew I needed to break free, but I did not know how. You never really know whether someone who threatens to kill themselves is bluffing until they cross the line. In my mind, the line kept getting closer and closer with every one of my boyfriend's desperate performances.

I realized that our relationship was toxic shortly after I ran away from home to move in with him. I was 16 years old and running from my parents' rules, only to find that life with him was not the fantasy I dreamed it would be. My parents had never wanted me to date him, but the more they tried to keep us apart, the closer I drew to him. They prayed over me and tried to talk some sense into me, but by then I was sleepwalking through life. I was so broken and numb to reality that my existence had become dull and tasteless. I did not care about me and I did not care about anyone else. The longer I stayed, the worse it got. Fear kept me paralyzed and most days all I could do to have peace was sleep. The weight of the relationship drained all of my energy. I felt guilty for hurting my parents and disappointing them and I felt guilty for wanting to leave him. I spiraled deeper into depression and lost more of myself every day, It became an accomplishment for me to get out of bed in the morning, and it was an extra-special day if I actually washed up and made myself look presentable. I stopped going to school altogether, so my dreams of being an actress and a singer were slowly fading away until finally, surrounded by the spirit of death, eternal sleep began to sound like an attractive option for me as well.

The day my boyfriend pulled that gun was the day I realized how hopelessly stuck I really was. I would have no peace while this man was alive and I would not know peace if he were dead, as he would surely haunt me from the grave if he ever did pull that trigger. Scared, defeated, and emotionally exhausted, I was finally willing to acknowledge just how bad I wanted out of this mess. I hated to prove that my family was right about him. I knew I would have to eat crow and apologize, but given the circumstances, crow sounded like a tasty treat.

We were alone that day, so I had an exclusive front-row seat for the show. With a calm expression, my boyfriend locked me in the room and then made me sit next to him as he loaded the gun. As the bullets clicked into place, my thoughts raced frantically. What was I going to do? How would I explain why his brains were splattered all over the wall to his family and the police? What if he turned the gun on me? What if the police thought it was my fault, or worse, that I pulled the trigger? I could not go to *jail*. I had never even seen the inside of a police station. I would surely lose what was left of my mind if he went through with this. I had always been a **good girl.** How had my life become so bad?

To his satisfaction, I cried hysterically and begged

him to cancel the "show." He eventually gave in and put the gun down, Like the transition from Dr. Jekyll to Mr. Hyde, a very different man suddenly emerged. He was apologetic, tender, and concerned for my well-being which was the man I fell in love with. He consoled me and told me in a somber voice that I could leave if I wanted to. He said he understood that I wanted to go home, and he was not going to try and stop me anymore. I felt a moment of panicked indecision. Was he serious, or was this just another test to see if I really loved him? This was a new script, and I didn't know my lines. I watched wordlessly as he opened the bedroom door for me to leave. He then picked up the gun and sat on the bed. For a few moments, I stood frozen, terrified, not knowing what move to make next. If I turned to walk away, was he going to shoot me in the back? If I managed to walk out the door, would I hear the gun go off as he shot himself?

Introduction

Or would I really, finally have the freedom to move forward with my life, leave this drama behind, and make a fresh start once and for all?

In the end, I realized there was only one real option. I would **make a run for freedom or die trying.** We lived on the 8th floor in a project building in Brooklyn. I was a long way from my home in the Bronx, but the train station was just a few blocks away. I knew that if I could get to the train, I would be safe. I walked slowly backward out of the room. He did not look up at me. His face was an expressionless mask; I could not read it, and couldn't waste time trying. I just had to make my move. Once out of the room, I headed slowly and quietly for the front door, listening intently for his heavy footsteps all the way. I knew that at any given moment, he could change his mind and come running to snatch me up in a fit of anger.

With my heart pounding, I made it out the front door and then to the elevator. Quickly realizing that I didn't want to wait around for the elevator, I walked directly to the staircase and ran for dear life. I ran as fast as my little legs could carry me, thinking that if he wasn't at my heels with that gun, he might be at his bedroom window, poised to take me out as I crossed the street. I was literally running for my life, flying out of the building and past his group of friends, who were congregated, as always, right outside. There was no time for goodbyes. I only hoped they would stop him if they saw him coming after me.

Heaving and panting, I finally made it to the train station. The train was not there. The wait was agonizing. I paced the floor up and down the station, watching for my train -- any train -- to come. I kept a wary watch on the station entrance and mentally planned an escape route that would require me to jump across the tracks if need be.

Introduction

After what seemed like an eternity, the train squealed into the station. It was not until I heard the whir and hiss of the doors safely closing behind me did I breathe a long sigh of relief. I knew I looked disheveled and crazy but I did not care. **I was alive! I had made it out alive!**

I sat on the hard train seat, in the quiet, reflecting on what had happened and thanking God that I took the chance to run and lived to tell about it. I wondered if my boyfriend was dead and if I would get a call from the police or find them waiting to question me by the time I made it home. It did not matter. Nothing mattered. *I had my life*. I was so close to death and so many women like me never make it out alive to tell the story. I could have been one of the statistics I read about. My parents could have had to bury their child and live broken-hearted forever. And for what? All of this madness over a boy? In that moment, I asked God for forgiveness for all the times

I prayed that I would fall asleep and never wake up. I thanked him for my life and I declared without a doubt that I wanted to live it, and live it to the fullest. I prayed, just as my parents had taught me, for God's strength and guidance to take my shattered life and show me how to put the pieces back together again. Then, for the first time in a long time, I was able to feel. Jolted from my apathy, I felt my hope returning. I could see a light at the end of the tunnel. If I could find the strength to run out of Satan's claws, then surely I could get back on track and create a life that was worth living.

The first question I had to answer on my road to redemption was, "how did I get here?" I needed to figure out what caused my self-esteem to become so damaged that I would compromise my values and stay in an abusive relationship instead of loving myself enough to leave the FIRST time my boyfriend disrespected me. It was time to heal and it was time to break free.

Setting the Intention

Self-esteem is a culmination of many variables in our lives, and its cultivation begins when we are children. It only takes a minute to encourage the heart of a child or tear them down, causing damage that may take years to undo. Everyone has a story. So many of us walk around with damaged pieces of our heart from the afflictions we have endured. We do our very best to keep moving forward past the pain to become productive citizens in the world but we are indeed the walking wounded. This book is a guide to help people heal from their emotional wounds and truly establish healthy self-esteem. My hope is that after applying the principles of this book to your life, you will experience greater joy, peace, and freedom to be all-the-way you and create the life of your heart's desire. Whatever pieces of you have been stolen or given away, it is time to take them back!

There are six fundamental principles that I believe are essential building blocks to establish authentic self-esteem that is unshakable in the face of life's challenges. Those principles are: healing the child within; owning your power; tapping the spirit within; the practice of forgiveness; defining success for yourself; and developing an attitude of gratitude, no matter what. When we have healthy self-esteem, it positions us to achieve greatness in our lives. Knowing our worth and having high expectations from life will propel us forward into the abundant life God had promised us.

I am not a doctor, but a friend. I have learned a great deal about how to build healthy self-esteem through

Introduction

20 years of studies from experts in the field of personal development and from my own spiritual growth. I went from having self-esteem so low that I became a victim of teen domestic violence, depressed with thoughts of suicide to becoming a national motivational speaker, and the Bald Beauty Queen of Self-Esteem. At the age of 25, I began to lose all of the hair on my body as a result of the autoimmune disease, Alopecia Universalis. Initially I was devastated, but by using the foundational principles I will share with you in this book, I was able to build my self-esteem up so much that I made history when I competed in a pageant bald and was crowned 2011 Mrs. Black North Carolina.

There is a quote by Richard Bach that says, "You teach best what you most need to learn." I have found that my life's work has proved this to be true. I know how to pull myself up out of the dark places of life, not only because I read about it but because I lived it. Marianne Williamson said it best in her book *A Return to Love*, "No one can help with anything like someone who has been through the pain themselves."

I am a student of life. I have been committed to my own personal growth ever since that defining moment when I was faced with the worst possible choice – and decided I wanted to live. In spite of my challenges, I have never lost hope. I realize now how precious life is, and that there is no reason good enough to wish for death. No matter how bad things seem, joy will be waiting for you one morning if you just hold on. This is the truth I have been inspired to share.

When the shift occurred inside of me and I made the decision to move from being a **victim** to a **victor**, my whole world opened up. A friend introduced me to "Tapping the Power Within." That was the first book

Introduction

written by inspirational speaker, New Thought spiritual teacher, author, and now television personality, Reverend Dr. Iyanla Vanzant. Her ministry changed my life, simply because I could relate to her pain and life experiences. She spoke my language at a time when everyone around me acted as if I was speaking gibberish instead of English. Her piercing insight provided the clarity that I needed in the face of depression and brokenness. Twenty years ago, I went to see Reverend Vanzant speak live at Aaron Davis Hall in New York City. The theme of her message was "Tell Your Story." I learned that there was a divine purpose to my story that could empower others and facilitate healing. I always remembered her words, which is why I am honored to document some of my life lessons through my testimony and share them with you in this book to the best off my recollection. They are deeply personal and some of the memories are not the most pleasant for me, but I chose them in order to fully illustrate each principal. It is not my intention to make anyone a villain by drudging up the past. All of these issues are water under the bridge but as the old cliché goes, "you can't know where you are going, until you know where you have been." Even through the pain, there is beauty that lies in the strength and humility I have acquired in my evolution into the woman I am now and I am yet becoming. This is the reality for each of us. My goal is to teach you how to look beyond the pain and dissect the experiences to uncover the pearl of wisdom that lies within each trial and victory.

I am excited about your journey. I encourage you to use the lined space provided as a workbook to take notes and journal through the emotions and memories that come up for you. This book will only be a source of entertainment if you don't commit to the self-work it calls for. But if you do the exercises I suggest at the end of

Introduction

each chapter, you will find the abundant life you have been waiting for has really just been waiting for you. Warriors like me are holding a space for you as you move forward, and we await your presence on this side of freedom!

With Love-For Love,

SANDRADUBOSE

Principle 1:

Healing the Inner Child

S

"Until you heal the wounds of your past,
you will continue to bleed into the future."

~ Iyanla Vanzant

Self-esteem is so personal. No one can take it from you, and no one can give it to you either. It is yours and you own it forever. You may have had experiences in life that had a negative impact on your self-esteem, but ultimately, when you are ready, you do not need to look anywhere else but inside of yourself to rebuild and replenish your confidence and feelings of self-worth. It is always within your reach.

The way we feel about ourselves begins to take shape from our early childhood experiences. Some of us have had many challenges to overcome, while others have been blessed with a great childhood feeling affirmed, nurtured, safe, loved, and happy.

What matters most isn't how you start, but how you finish. In the book, *In the Heart of a Child, One Moment Can Last Forever,* Wess Stafford talks about how tender and impressionable the heart of a child is. He compares a child's spirit to wet cement or moist clay, just waiting for an act of kindness, a hug, or a well-timed word of encouragement to mold it into something great. Understanding the weight of our impact and deliberately spreading seeds of love is a gift we can all give to the next generation. This first principle, Healing the Inner Child, is all about reflecting back on our childhood experiences and finding the pain points that are unresolved and in need of healing so that we can finally move forward. We must perform a self-evaluation and deal with the skeletons in our closet because if we don't, we will come home one day to find them having a wild party in our living rooms!

Church Girl Blues

I was born and raised as a Pentecostal Christian. From the time I was six months old, my family attended church every Sunday. That was normally an all-day event, and there was service on Wednesday nights and Fridays as well. My dad was a deacon in the church, and he was responsible for helping to take up the collection of tithes and offerings, leading the devotional service of praise and worship, and supporting the pastor when he traveled as a guest speaker both locally and out of state. My father was the spiritual head of our family, and we followed his example.

In our church, women were required to wear their heads covered with a hat, a doily or fashionable head covering of their choice during service. Women were not allowed to wear pants, sleeveless shirts, or open-toe shoes. Makeup, nail polish, and jewelry other than a wedding band and watch to tell the time, were also forbidden fruits. We could not have our ears pierced or even cut our hair to sport the latest styles. All of these things were viewed as "worldly," and we were taught that God's desire was for us to live righteous and look holy. We wore skirts every day that went past the knee -- even in the dead of winter. We were not supposed to listen to secular music or even celebrate Christmas with a tree and presents like the world did. All the fun things I wanted to do were seemingly "against our religion." As a child, I never could rationalize why God would send a woman to hell just for wearing a pair of pants, or why he would give me such a passion for all kinds of music and only allow me to listen to gospel music without feeling guilty and sinful. Was it really that serious? And if it was such a crime, then why did every-one else in the world seem to get away with it? I felt unlucky and I resented having to follow these rules when none of my friends had to. I wanted to be cool and fit in with everyone else. Instead my young, free spirit felt chained to the old rugged cross, just like the words in the song we sang during devotion.

My elementary school days were filled with ques-tions from schoolmates of why I dressed the way I did. "Don't you get cold?" they would ask on snowy winter days. "I wear skirts because the Bible says that women should not wear clothing pertaining to a man," I would reply. I repeated verbatim what my parents told me to say, even if I did not believe it myself. My commitment to skirts was good news to the boys who kept dropping pen-cils underneath the desk to try and sneak a peek. Wearing skirts put me in a vulnerable position and I stuck out like a sore thumb -- or better yet, like the thumb I got teased for fervently sucking until I was 12 years old. I only took my thumb out of my mouth to talk, eat, and brush my teeth. My extreme buck teeth bore witness to that fact. But thank goodness for braces!

We attended a small church and the majority of the congregation was made up of the pastor's children and family members. There was no separate morning service for children in place, so the kids sat through the regular service with their parents. I took many a good nap leaning on my mother's lap while the preacher was preaching. Church services were uplifting and the Holy Ghost made regular appearances. The choir selections were my favorite part. I was always awake for those! The choir sang their hearts out until the energy was high and ripe for the visitation of the spirit, which would cause folk to jump, shout, run, and dance around from the internal fire they experienced. Wide-eyed, I took in all the antics, which I found entertaining and comical as a kid. I could not wait to go home and practice the jerks, facial expressions, and funky foot action I had witnessed. I had a few personal favorite shout moves that I perfected, however, no matter how hard I tried, I could never emulate the words that were spoken in other tongues. "Don't play with Jesus!" my older sister would say. "You keep it up and he's going to get inside of you and you will be shouting for real." The thought of that would be enough to make me sit down. I was scared of the Holy Ghost, so the joke was over. I had enough reasons to feel uncomfortable about church, so the last thing I wanted was to fall out on the floor and have what I perceived to be at that time, a scary out-of-body experience.

I had an awful habit as a child of having to use the

bathroom frequently. I don't know why, but no matter how much or how little I drank, I could not seem to hold liquid. I felt the sensation on my bladder and I needed to let it go. Admittedly, it was quite frustrating for my parents. Traveling with me on long trips was especially nightmarish. I was no stranger to peeing in a cup when we went on those long 12-hour drives from New York City to South Carolina to visit with family in the summer. I have had numerous embarrassing moments in school and on school trips from not quite making it to the bathroom in time. I was traumatized regularly!

One typical Sunday when I was around eight years old, my mom excused me from my seat to make my normal rounds to the potty during the praise and worship part of service. Proper church etiquette required that once the preaching began, all traffic must stop and everyone was to be seated in quiet reverence for the word of God. I wanted to reverence the Word, but as the pastor began to preach, I felt that strong urge to tinkle again. I whispered softly in her ear:

"Mom, I need to use the bathroom again."

"No, you already went to the bathroom. The preacher is preaching, so you have to wait until he is finished," she whispered back to me.

I heard the words that came out of her mouth, but that did not stop me from feeling uncomfortable. I started wiggling around in my seat praying that God would take the sensation away. I waited a few minutes for that miracle, but it didn't come. I knew I had reached my bathroom quota, but I sincerely needed to go again.

"Mom, I really have to go to the bathroom," I said.

My mom had a very low tolerance for foolishness. Compassion was not her strong suit, discipline was.

"I said no! You already have been to the bathroom. Now you sit there and hold it until he is finished preaching! You can wait. " She really believed it was that simple.

I knew it did not make sense to her and it did not make sense to me either. I would have loved to have been able to hold it and avoid pissing momma off in church, but this one was a red alert. It was no time for momma to be stubborn. If she knew what I knew, she would let me tip toe my little self quietly down those stairs to the bath-room. I wished the Lord would have given her a heads up because she was not listening to me.

My mom was not budging from her final answer. Meanwhile, my very life was flashing before my eyes. The church was filled with people, and we sat on long wooden benches with smooth, shellacked surfaces and no dividers between the seats.

I will never forget that day. The air conditioner wasn't working, so the sanctuary was very warm. I looked around at all the adults, who sat dressed in their Sunday best, fanning themselves with paper fans that were stapled to flat wooden sticks and had funeral parlors advertised on them. All of the church doors were open in the hopes of catching a breeze from the street. The flies would stop in to hear the good word so they could buzz it all around town. The adults were listening intently with shouts of amen and hallelujah as the preacher started stirring things up. My dad was sitting in his usual spot, in the front pew close to the pulpit so he could be in position to take up the offering, which came around several times throughout the service. The building fund offering would provide for the church's necessities, like the new air conditioner we desperately needed. I could not make eye contact with my dad and convince him to come rescue me. All I could see was the back of his little head, which resembled my own.

Mommy the Warden had a close watch on me and the look in her eyes let me know that my bathroom trip was not up for discussion. I had no one to turn to and I could not take the pain anymore. I did the only thing I could do… I sat there and I peed.

There was the familiar feeling of warm urine flowing though my pretty dress. It formed a puddle behind me and slowly began to inch down the pew, spreading the wealth to the lucky people that happen to be sitting in my row. I was mortified and terrified! I whispered to my mother as my tears began to fall apologetically from my face, "Mommy, I peed." She looked at me in disbelief, so I scooted up a bit to expose my dilemma. The pee began to roll faster to the right side and my mom quietly caught the attention of the people on our row gesturing for them to move up before the urine train got to their stop. I was crying my eyes out by this time, and my mother was embarrassed and furious. She got the attention of the ushers, who quickly gathered paper towels to stop the train. The children in the church began to snicker at me and the adults looked at me with disgust. They could all rest assured that my momma was going to handle me and handle me well! She grabbed me by one arm and escorted me down the steps to the bathroom. I wished she would have let me visit just three minutes before then. Maybe then I would have had the chance to live to see my next birthday! Momma took me into the bathroom stall and angrily spanked my wet bottom. I was sorry on so many levels. I cried and said, "I told you I had to go to the bathroom!"

The doctors never found an issue with my bladder, so my mother was confounded as to why I had to go all the time. She would always ask me, but I had no answers. I was devastated and wished I could just disappear. I was constantly embarrassed and I felt like I could not do anything right. All I wanted to know was, "Why me Lord?"

My parent's religious views evolved soon after I became a teenager, and we left that church along with many of the rules we followed behind. My mom finally let me have my ears pierced and allowed me to wear light colored nail polish and jewelry. She even bought me some new clothes including my very first pair of pants! I was so excited and I felt a sense of freedom with the ability to express myself in a brand new way, without feeling sinful. I made my pants debut at the roller skating rink for my junior high school senior trip. My friends in school could not believe their eyes as I stood there feeling like a runway model in my baggy red pants and white long sleeved shirt. They hovered around in awe giving me compliments and admiring my new style. That was a great moment in my life, and my confidence grew instantly because I finally felt accepted by my peers and for the first time, I was even considered a little bit cool.

Pause For Reflection

I want to pause here for a moment to allow you to reflect on your childhood. Think about what memories and feelings came up for you while reading the story. Write about them on the pages provided.

Answering the following five questions will help jog your memory and get you focused.

What is your fondest childhood memory, good or bad?

_____

_____

_____

_____

_____

_____

_____

_____

_____

_____

_____

_____

_____

What was your elementary school experience like?

_____

_____

_____

_____

_____

_____

_____

_____

_____

_____

_____

Were there specific people that you felt really built you up or tore you down as a child?

_____

_____

_____

_____

_____

_____

_____

_____

_____

_____

_____

How did that impact your beliefs about

yourself?

_____

_____

_____

_____

_____

_____

_____

_____

_____

_____

_____

What negative experience are you still holding on to that needs to be resolved?

_____

_____

_____

_____

_____

_____

_____

_____

_____

_____

You Can Run but You Can't Hide

I got married on a hot summer day in August of 1995 when I was 21 years old. We had a beautiful wedding ceremony and reception, both of which were held at a catering hall in the Bronx. About 100 of our closest family and friends attended and the event went smoothly as planned. It was a wonderful day just like the fairytale all princesses dream of. The very next day, we left for our honeymoon to Nassau in the Bahamas. We returned home after one week as happily married newlyweds -- no longer live-in boyfriend and girlfriend. All of the festivities and planning were over and our real life as husband and wife had begun.

One romantic evening shortly into our marriage, I had an awful experience while attempting to enjoy some intimate time with my husband. All of a sudden, I became panicked and overcome with fear. I started kicking and screaming, and told him to get away from me as if I did not know him at all. It was as if something snapped inside of my mind. I had never experienced anything like that before. I started crying hysterically for no apparent reason. Fearing that I may have had a nervous breakdown, my husband consoled me as best as he could. When I finally calmed down, I apologized for my outburst, but my heart suddenly felt heavy with a sense of grief and I did not know why. That feeling stayed there, consuming me, for months. I could not shake it, nor could I experience intimacy anymore without becoming very emotional. I had no desire for my husband and I felt guilty about it. He loved me enough to be patient and understanding as I tried to work through the sudden meltdown, which was a horrible way to start off a marriage.

I began to pray for God to reveal to me the source of the heavy emotions I was suddenly carrying around, which had created a distance between me and my husband. The answers were revealed to me through my dreams, in stages, like pieces of a giant jigsaw puzzle I had to spread out and put together. I would wake up in the middle of the night confused, remembering just fragments of a scene that seemed familiar, but I could not quite make it out yet. Each dream brought me slowly closer to clarity, preparing me gently for what was to come. Finally, one morning I awoke from my dreams and I understood it all. I remembered. I did not have all of the pieces, but I had enough to make out the secret that had never been told and stayed trapped inside of my subconscious mind ever since I was seven years old.

There lay the memory of an inappropriate touch, and feelings of confusion and fear. The trigger in my mind was set off, connecting back to the weight of a family friend who molested me one day when I was a little girl, which altered my life forever. Apparently, I blocked it from my mind and hid it deep within my subconscious, even from myself. I finally understood why I acted out in ways that I did as a child and a teenager. I uncovered the buried source of pain and I realized how that festering wound infected my self-esteem like poison over the years.

After the revelation I received through my dreams, it took some time for me to settle into my new reality and manage all of the emotions that had surfaced. I was on a rollercoaster of anger, hatred, sorrow, and regret. I wished I could go back and undo some of the things I had done. I even wanted revenge, but realistically there was nothing I could ever do that would compensate for the damage that had been done. The past was the past, but since I never dealt with it, it was bleeding into my future.

I connected the dots back to my childhood days of growing up in church and how it had a profound effect on me in so many ways. I learned that God is omnipresent, but the forces of evil can be anywhere, in our family and even inside the church walls. You can find it lurking on any row, in any place of worship regardless of the religion. Where there are people, there will be pain. Where there is pain, there will be problems. My problem of an overactive bladder had more to do with my mental and emotional state of mind than my liquid intake. I have since figured out that I have the urge to use the bathroom a lot more when I am uncomfortable or really nervous, even as an adult. I understand now why I had to pee so many times when I was in church as a child.

There was a man there whose presence made me very uncomfortable. Just the sound of his voice weighed heavy on my bladder as a constant reminder of the day he took the little light of mine and caused it not to shine. I never spoke a word about what happened to anyone because I was afraid. I kept it to myself but I learned later in life that I was not the only child he victimized when he was alive. Deeply rooted issues will inevitably sprout up like weeds, just as secret sins committed will one day be judged by heavenly authorities. Meanwhile, the universal law of karma prevails and no one is exempt or invincible.

The handwriting was on the wall throughout my life, but no one stopped to read it. All the skeletons I kept locked away in my mind's closet fell out and landed right in my bedroom soon after I said "I do." I thought I ran from that pain for years, but it finally tackled me and I realized it was right beside me, slowing me down all along

The Facts of the Matter

I know that many of you who will read this book will unfortunately also be victims of some form of sexual abuse. During my healing process, as I worked through my emotions, I began to share my story with close friends that I trusted. To my surprise, nearly 80% of the women I knew responded with the same two words: "ME TOO!" It was practically unanimous: nearly all of us had experienced abuse in our lives, which was a frightening reality. Why is sexual abuse such a common thread, especially amongst women? Too many women are subsequently carrying around emotional baggage and acting out on unresolved issues that they may have kept secret for years. Even worse, they may have told someone who did not believe them or simply swept it under the rug, leaving the victims to continually bear the burden or endure the act. According to the Rape, Abuse & Incest National Network:

- Someone in the U.S. is sexually assaulted every 2 minutes.

- 44% of the victims are under age 18.

- 54% of sexual assaults are not reported to the police.

- Approximately 2/3 of assaults are committed by someone known to the victim.

It is a hard pill to swallow, but these are the facts in our society. As parents, we have to protect our children by being conscious of that reality and discerning of the adults that we allow them to be alone with. It's not a cause to be paranoid, but it is important to be aware and pay attention. We have to create a safe space so that children will be comfortable enough to let us in and share even the ugly or hurtful things that happen in their lives knowing that we will protect them.

Sexual abuse is an example I use from my life to illustrate this principle, but your situation could be any number of things. So where does it hurt? Only you know what the issues are that started way back when and are still weighing you down today. Was it a parent who was not there for you because of neglect, death, or divorce? Was it a sibling rivalry or a challenge with other family members? Was it drugs or alcohol abuse? How about physical, mental or verbal abuse? Did you endure excessive teasing, bullying, or wrestle with weight and self-image issues?

I could ride this elevator up all day long, so just stop me when I get to your floor because no matter what the reason, all pain is simply pain.

"Someone was hurt before you; wronged before you;
beaten before you; humiliated before you;
raped before you; yet, someone

SURVIVED."

~ Maya Angelou

Pep Talk

Everyone has a past. This exercise is designed to help you look back, identify the problem areas in your life, and then begin the healing process. There are no quick fixes or overnight successes. Healing is a process and you need to be gentle with yourself. Be your own advocate and rally behind yourself in a brand new way. As breakthrough specialist, author, and inspirational speaker, Lisa Nichols, says, **"Personal transformation is NOT a Google download. Unfortunately, there is no APP for it "** Trust me, I already checked. All you can do is start by heading in the right direction and take one loving step at a time.

Warning: You may find that some deeply rooted issues require more work than just talking to a trusted friend or journaling through them. If this is the case for you, then be honest with yourself. Sometimes you get to a point in life where you're forced to admit that you need help. If you could fix the issue on your own, you would have fixed it already, so don't waste any more time lying to yourself. Everyone needs help sometime and only the truly strong people are the ones who make themselves vulnerable enough to ask for the help they need. Cowards are the ones who are too afraid to face the truth and admit that they are stuck in a rut. This is not a time for cowardice. You have to be sick and tired of being sick and tired of yourself. That is when you will be hungry enough to change. Personal freedom is not FREE and it has never been! There is a price to pay so cash in your ego right now and focus on the big picture. You know you want to get to the other side of the mountain, but every time you try to climb up to get over, you slip down. We have all been there at some point and that is the time when you call for a boost up or some shoulders to stand on to give you leverage. Seek out help if you need it from a psychologist, a clinical social worker, a therapist, or even a support group. There is NO SHAME in soliciting help and it is never too late. The shame is when you insanely keep doing the same thing over year after year while expecting a different result. It's time to do a NEW thing!

Second Warning: Be aware that some people in your life may not understand the process, so don't wait for every one's approval to get healthy. You do not need their blessing to heal; it is a personal decision and only you know what you really need. Don't let the fear of judgment cloud you from seeing things clearly and taking the steps you need to take to move forward. It's your self-esteem, remember? Now act like you own it!

Healing Exercise

Managing the Stinking-Thinking: Some of us unconsciously have negative beliefs about ourselves that we
play over in our minds like a broken record. We may not
even realize how embedded those thoughts are. We have
to deliberately reprogram our minds and replenish them
with thoughts of truth and love. I want you to stay alert
and start paying attention to what is going on inside of
you. Begin listening to your inner self-talk, and if you find
that you spend more time beating yourself down than
building yourself up, try this exercise to counteract the
negativity with affirmations that will shine a light into
those dark areas.

1. Get two sheets of paper and write numbers 1 through 10 on each. Name one "THE LIES" and the other "THE TRUTH." On the LIES sheet, write down the top ten negative things that you say to yourself that are not life-affirming and keep you stuck in the past. Hopefully you can trace those thoughts back to their origin and see that you have been unconsciously perpetuating the lies you were told. No matter where they began, it's time to put them to an end. Some examples of unhealthy thoughts: I am not going to amount to anything; no one loves me; I am stupid; I am worthless; I am ugly; I can't do anything right.

2. Now, on the TRUTH sheet, write a positive affirmation to counteract each negative one with words that empower you and adds to your life force. Create affirmations that speak directly to your pain points. Hang it up in a visible location like your bathroom or bedroom mirror.

Recite these positive affirmations EVERY DAY whether you feel them or not. Look at yourself in the mirror lovingly just as you would someone else you care about. Encourage yourself with those words. Some examples of healthy thoughts: I can be anything I want to be in life; God loves me; I am smart and capable; I am worthy of all good things; I am beautiful inside and out; I am learning and growing every day.

"Death and life are in the power of the tongue."
~Proverbs 18:21 KJV.

Speak life to yourself and commit your affirmations to memory. Use them as your weapons to fight the negative thoughts when they kick in. Research shows that it takes at least 21 days to create a new habit, so be consistent and diligent. Pretty soon those words will have taken root, blossomed like a garden in your heart, and become your new beliefs.

Use these blank pages as your safe place to purge and get your feelings out of your head and on to some paper. It can help you manage your emotions and feel lighter.

<u>Journal Question:</u>

What did you learn about yourself and how did you feel while doing the affirmation exercise?

_____

_____

_____

_____

_____

_____

_____

_____

_____

_____

_____

_____

_____

_____

_____

_____

_____

_____

_____

_____

_____

_____

_____

_____

_____

_____

_____

_____

_____

My Crown and Glory

_____

_____

_____

_____

_____

_____

_____

_____

_____

_____

_____

_____

_____

_____

_____

_____

_____

Principle 2:

Owning Your Power

S

"God, grant me the serenity to accept the things
I cannot change;

Courage to change the things I can;

And wisdom to know the difference."

~The Serenity Prayer by *Reinhold Niebuhr*

No one is exempt from the trials of life. We were all created and born in the same way, and our journey here on earth will inevitably end at the appointed time for each of us. In between our arrival and our departure, we will have experiences that are meant to help us become more of who we were predestined to be, *if* we consciously extract the lesson. Along the road, there will be moments of joy, sorrow, pain, and victory. Each hill and valley is customized and specially made to meet our individual needs. It does not serve us to ask "why me?" or compare ourselves to others because life is not one-size-fits-all. Your life is especially made to fit the contours of your personality and meet the needs required for the fulfillment of your destiny. There are no mistakes.

In Principle 2, we will look at how we can awaken to and own the power we possess to create the life we desire, by becoming masters of our mind. There is always a silver lining in even the most challenging of situations, but you must adjust your vision and perception to see it. Once you shift your attitude you can begin to create a life of great magnitude.

The Milestone

On April 3, 1999, I turned 25 years old. This birthday felt like a milestone for me and I really wanted to celebrate it. I had been married for almost 4 years by then and Miyah, our first baby girl, had just turned 1 year old a month prior. I had a lot to be thankful for, and since no one in my inner circle felt inclined to throw a party for me, I decided to put a dinner party together for myself. Somehow I knew intuitively that year would be a turning point in my life and I was determined to bring it in with a bang!

As part of my birthday present wish list from my loved ones, I received a gift certificate to a full day at the spa. I had never been to one before and turning 25 seemed like the perfect opportunity to treat myself like a big girl. I got a manicure, pedicure, full body massage, and facial done at an exclusive salon in Manhattan. Overall, it was a nice experience -- except for the facial extractions. When you see people relaxing in spas on TV, you never see the part where they practically twist your nose off of your face and press deep into your pores with a metal contraption. I came to relax and have cucumbers put on my eyes, not to end up in a headlock! Had I known my face would be red and swollen by the time it was over, I would not have scheduled my birthday celebration for that same evening.

Big Girl Lesson Number 1: After a facial with extractions, wait a day or two for your face to go back to normal before you do appearances. The swollen face look is not cute!

My Crown and Glory

That night I met a few of my closest friends and family at Tony's Di Napoli, a popular Italian restaurant in New York City. The dinner was lovely and I was very happy breaking bread and sharing laughs with the people that I love most. It was one of the best birthdays ever. A couple of days prior, I got my hair done and it looked beautiful. I had them do my signature short precision cut, which was similar to the style of R & B Singer Anita Baker. It was tapered at the neck and the curls were feathered and layered to perfection. Everyone complimented me on my hair that night, but they kept pointing out a small bald patch behind my right ear. It was smooth, perfectly round, and about the size of the tip of my finger. I had no idea that it was even there. My girlfriends and I came to the conclusion that my hairdresser must have nicked me with the clippers when I got my hair cut and failed to tell me. *Okay, no big deal. It will grow back in, I thought.* I was certainly not going to get my panties in a bunch about it and ruin my night. The only big deal that night was diving into the birthday cake my friends brought for me from Valencia, my favorite bakery. I guess my friends and family caught on to all of my not-so-subtle hints and made sure that my sweet tooth was taken care of for my special day. From sunup to sundown, I welcomed in 25 and stepped boldly into a brand new chapter in my life.

My Crown and Glory

Hair Care

The week following the party found me babysitting my bathroom mirror, using a hand mirror to look at the back of my head. That weird little bald spot was starting to grow bigger every day. It was odd because there was no breakage, just smooth skin like the skin on the back of my hand. No hair was sticking out of it, and even the follicles seemed to have disappeared overnight. My scalp did not itch or have any redness. I had no idea what was going on or why this was happening to me. I made an appointment to see my primary care physician and went in right away. After an examination, he told me that my hair loss was caused by an autoimmune disease. In autoimmune diseases, the immune system mistakenly attacks the body's own organs and tissues. In this case my body was attacking my hair follicles, causing bald patches. While there were treatments available that could possibly stimulate hair growth, there was unfortunately no cure.

The only thing I knew about autoimmune disease was what I had learned from my father's experience with Lupus just a few years prior. Given my family history, I was not only afraid of losing my hair, I was afraid that I would get a disease that would make me really sick and compromise the quality of my life. The doctor gave me a referral for a dermatologist and the nurse made an appointment for me right away. The goal was for them to start me on any available treatments immediately before any more hair fell out. I was frightened and confused, but optimistic. I did not know what to expect, but I was willing to try anything. The bald spot was becoming more noticeable and if the hair did not start to grow back in soon, I would have to find new ways to cover it up. If worse came to worst, I would have to start wearing a wig!

My Crown and Glory

My first visit to the dermatologist was pretty traumatic. By the day of my visit, there was already a new small bald patch taking form in a different section of my scalp. It was as if the hair fairy came overnight and took patches of hair from my scalp as I slept, but did not leave me any money. While waiting for the doctor to enter the room, I perused the pamphlets on the wall and read about the different types of hair loss and treatments. I had the first kind, called *alopecia areata* (Years later after having a scalp biopsy I was diagnosed with *Central Centrifugal Cicatricial Alopecia (CCCA)* as well). Alopecia Areata causes unpredictable patchy hair loss in spots on the scalp, but the hair is likely to grow back after a while. Apparently nearly 5 million people in the United States alone had my condition, even though I had never heard of it or met anyone else who did. The next type was called *alopecia totalis,* where you lose all of the hair on your scalp only.

Then the rarest kind was *alopecia universalis*, where people could actually lose all of the hair on their scalp, face and body, even down to the nose hairs. I shuddered at the thought and felt happy to be at the doctor's office so he could fix this situation before it got out of hand.

The doctor was very kind and compassionate, but his needle was not. I was prepared to use topical ointments of steroid cream and rub into my bald spots for a few weeks. I was not prepared for the more aggressive treatment of steroids injected directly into my scalp. It was a lot to take in at the moment, but I did what I had to do. He numbed the bald areas before the procedure, but watching him come toward me with a needle to my head was traumatizing. It was bad enough to have to manage these new feelings of insecurity about my hair loss, but to be further subjected to the pain of a needle pricking me several times in my head felt like an awful punishment.

Tears rolled down my face as the doctor worked away at my scalp, going as gently and quickly as he could. I held myself together, remembering how my daddy always told me I was a tough cookie. Unfortunately, I didn't feel like one in that moment.

Harsh Reality

When you have been diagnosed with any disease it is difficult to resist the temptation to Google it and find out what the worst case scenario could be. It is important to be an informed patient, but sometimes too much information can cause unnecessary anxiety. I had to know more about this autoimmune disease that was stripping away my confidence with every wayward strand. I took to the World Wide Web in search of answers and comfort from others who may be going through the same experience. Instead I found websites and articles with pictures that made my stomach hurt with fear. I saw photos of people young and old, of all races, with differing forms of alopecia. Some had scalps that looked diseased, with big patches of hair missing. Their heads reminded me of a globe with islands surrounded by bodies of water. Others had scalps that were completely bald! I could not decide which was worse. Many of the people in the photos had no eyebrows, eyelashes, or hair anywhere, and my heart went out to them. My heart broke in half when I saw pictures of little bald children who looked like they were going through chemotherapy even though they weren't.

I was grateful that this disease did not start for me when I was a child. I don't know how I would have managed that with all of my other issues. Teasing, bullying, and low self-esteem are common issues for children with alopecia. Managing sports and physical activities, like gym class, cheerleading or karate, become a nightmare for a child that chooses to wear wigs so they will fit in. The looming fear of mean kids pulling off the wig for entertainment becomes a just cause for homeschooling, and dating is just an additional source of stress. Being forced to look different can either make you stronger or break you down. In that moment, I was leaning on the broken side. I had some patchy hair loss and I was petrified at the thought of becoming one of the totally bald people posing in the pictures. I pleaded with God in prayer. *Oh God please, don't let that happen to me! I couldn't handle that Lord. This is not fair. Don't you think I have been through enough in my life already? I will do anything God, just PLEASE don't let me lose all of my hair!* I waited for an answer.

He gave me strength.

I prayed for healing.

He granted me patience.

Wigging Out

Weeks and months went by and even though I continued to go back to the dermatologist for injections regularly, the hair was still falling out and forming new bald spots in other areas of my scalp. I had no choice but to wear wigs and I hated every minute of it. I found out that the size of my head was ultra- petite, so average-sized wigs did not fit me properly. Wigs looked like helmets on me. They were itchy and hot and I lived in fear of them falling off in public every day. No matter which wig store I went to, I could rarely find a decent wig to fit me or my budget. Custom made wigs ran upwards of $1000, with little or no help from health insurance companies to offset the cost. They were not an option for me and my family. Out of desperation, I was forced to pay money I did not necessarily have to purchase a wig I didn't even like. The most difficult part was feeling as though I was not being my-self. Every day I put on a new persona along with the hair to help me cope, and every day I felt like a fake version of myself, while the real Sandra was hidden from the world. I could not wait to go home after work just so I could snatch my wig off, throw it on my dresser and be free at last.

Big Girl Lesson Number 2: Life does not stop and wait for you to get all of your personal issues worked out be-fore it resumes. No matter what you are feeling or going through, you have to set those feelings aside and still take care of your responsibilities to get through the day. I did not get a special free pass because of my trials. Everyone is going through something, and this is my particular cross to bear.

Each day I put on my wig that felt like an oversized dunce cap, did my makeup, and resumed with business as usual. Eventually my frustration began to turn into a silent depression, and every day I had to fight not to let it win. I prayed that no one at work would comment on or look too hard at my hair. In reality, most people honestly did not know that I was wearing a wig. I chose a style that was similar to the way I normally wore my hair so the transition was smooth. But to me, my wig couldn't have been more obvious. I was very embarrassed by it, and my insecurity drove me crazy. I was convinced that people were talking to me, but keeping their eyes focused on my hair trying to figure out if it was real. I was no longer comfortable talking to people, and if anyone complimented my hair, I would want to run to the bathroom and cry in the stall, convinced they were making fun of me. They may have been sincere, but I was so uncomfortable in my skin that I could not even receive a compliment. As far as I was concerned, anything positive about my hair could only be a lie. My perception of myself created a miserable reality.

Six months after my initial breakout, I decided to give up on the steroid injections that were obviously not working for me. Six months later, with only 50% of the hair on my scalp left, the alopecia went into remission and my hair finally began to grow back. I was so excited! I decided to stay natural and grow beautiful dreadlocks. 95 % of it grew back. There were a few small bald spots, but I could live with that, and living certainly became easier now that I had enough hair to take off my wig. I loved my locks, and as they matured into permanent twists they grew to shoulder length. I felt like my old self again, but even better.

Surviving The Fall

When Elajah, my second daughter, was born, the adjustment of having two children caused a shock to my system. After managing her regular late night crying sessions as an infant, I was completely exhausted and sleep-deprived. For many women, the onset of autoimmune diseases occurs during child-bearing years. It can be triggered by high levels of stress, trauma, or major changes in hormone levels, like those that occur during pregnancy and childbirth. By the time Elajah was one year old, my alopecia had returned, and this time it was aggressive.

One by one my lovely locks fell to the floor, a little every day starting from the crown of my head. I would lift my hair for a ponytail and lose a lock like a leaf falling from a tree. I felt as though I was in the autumn of my life and the threat of going bald loomed ahead as the inevitable winter. My eyebrows were thinning and missing spots. I would pull my eyelashes and they would fall out painlessly in between my fingers. Even hair in my private areas began to disappear overnight. I thought I was going crazy because it seemed so surreal. I would wake up thinking, "I could have sworn I had some hair there yesterday!" I knew that eventually, there would not be a trace left of hair anywhere on my body.

My husband, family, and friends were as supportive as possible, but it was scary for all of us. I needed support from someone who personally understood what the experience was like. I went back on to those alopecia websites and found some chat rooms for people with alopecia. It was like having a virtual group therapy session. In the chat room, everyone says their name, how long they have had alopecia, and shares their story or questions. I wanted to hear what others had to say and it gave me comfort to know I was not alone. I would read everything they wrote, but never chime in. I was so hurt; I wasn't ready to talk about my condition. I felt like I was sitting outside the circle listening, but at least I was in the room.

I revisited the pictures of the people with alopecia universalis that originally scared me. This time I had more compassion for those people because I was now one of them. However, I was angry about my alopecia. I did not want to be in the "bald club," and I did not understand why the people in the pictures were smiling. Did they think this crap was fun or funny? They were dancing and celebrating themselves at the patient conference as if they did not care that they were bald. *Who does stuff like that?* I thought. Maybe they knew something I didn't know because from where I was sitting, having my beautiful locks falling to the floor was no laughing matter!

I'm Every Woman

I was losing my battle with alopecia miserably. The hair loss was gaining on me and the hole at the top of my head had grown so big that I could not cover it up with a pony-tail anymore. Up until that point, I could arrange every lock to lay in a perfect row to cover up that bald spot. Now I no longer had enough hair left to camouflage it. I became increasingly self-conscious, and I felt uncomfort-able if anyone stared at me for too long. I was torn be-tween waiting with hopes that the bald spots would soon grow or just taking matters into my own hands and cutting all of my hair off.

Eventually I felt as though I had sung the same old sad song long enough. My hair was falling out more each day no matter what I did. If it was all going to fall out anyway, then why was I torturing myself by waiting around? I was ready to move on and start living again instead of being constantly consumed by a situation I could not change or control. I wanted to have a new conversation about any topic other than hair loss. It was time for me to refocus my prayer life on more important issues in my life, rather than begging for my hair to grow back every night. I got tired of feeling anxious about the issue and I desperately needed to get to a sincere place of peace and serenity. *Out of my desperate need for a change, I woke up and recognized my own power.* Maybe the bald people on the website were smiling and happy because they did not have to worry about hair anymore. They were free and I was still in bondage, consumed with thoughts of hair follicles. I wanted to dance and feel what they were feeling. Whether I liked it or not, I was one of them. I knew they did not ask to join the "bald club" either, but they were making the best of it.

The truth was that when I got good and ready to move forward, I could literally end my own torture and step into freedom simply by adopting a NEW ATTITUDE. *I could not make my hair come back, but I had the power to change my mind and reassign the value I had placed on this hair loss experience by shifting my perspective.* The experience could only be as deep and painful as I allowed it to be. *I could **choose** to continue to obsess about the hair loss or I could **decide** that it was not going to be my top priority anymore or stop me from feeling good about myself.* I was in great health otherwise and at the end of the day I had a lot to be grateful for because things could always be worse.

My family and friends were awesome and my husband was truly amazing. He was and still is my solid rock throughout the entire alopecia experience. He never looked at me any differently and continued to declare his love for me daily and confirm how beautiful I still was in his eyes. I wanted to believe him, but I could not see that beauty for myself or accept the unconditional love that was being offered to me. Even when I withdrew, he never did, and when I was ready, his love was always right there.

Big Girl Lesson #3: No one can give you self-esteem, even if they tell you you're beautiful all day, every day. Your sincere opinion of yourself cannot be based upon what others think of you. It is derived from a clear under-standing of who you are and your value in spite of any challenges you may be going through. Learn how to be your own best friend and advocate for you the way you would for someone else. Have compassion for that person staring back at you in the mirror, because you need you more than anyone else in the world. Focus on connecting with you and giving yourself unconditional love. The more you love you, the more love you will have to give and be able to receive from other people.

I made the decision to cut the rest of my hair off instead of waiting for it to all fall out. My husband offered to do it for me, but I really wanted to do it myself. It felt like a rite of passage, and it held a deep symbolic meaning for me. It was a personal threshold that I was crossing and my initiation into "the bald club" of happy dancing people who were truly free. I was a warrior, and I felt as though after all I had already been through in my life, if I could do this, I could do anything!

My mother-in-law lived downstairs from us in the two-family-house we resided in. She lives with the auto-immune disease Scleroderma. It causes a hardening of the skin, and in some cases it impacts the internal organs as well. Her illness started when she was in her child-bearing years, so she understood personally how it felt as a woman to endure changes to your body image that are caused by disease. It was great support for me to see how well she managed her condition. She never had public pity parties and you never heard her complain or give up the fight.

The day I cut off my hair, my husband was at work and my oldest daughter was in school. I was home alone with the baby, so I asked her to come upstairs and sit with me while I did the deed.

I was ready to take my freedom back, but I needed some theme music to set it off. I reached for Whitney Houston's version of "I'm Every Woman" and I turned the volume up high. I felt like a boxer walking into the arena with an entourage and some theme music to get me pumped up. I was dancing around the living room preparing my mind for the stick and moves I was about to put on this hair loss situation. Alopecia was going down and I was not afraid of my opponent. I was done crying and, as Whitney sang, I was every woman and all I needed to complete this task was in me! I guess it looked like I was doing a war dance. I was reaching deep into my soul calling on the strength of my ancestors to take the chains from around my mind, my heart, and my life with every swish of my hips. My mother-in-law felt the whole dramatic scene to be comical. She sat there holding Elajah looking at me curiously as if her chicken was in the oven and she wanted me to hurry up so she could get back to it.

"Is all of that really necessary?" she asked as she laughed at me. "YES," I said! "It is necessary!" I felt like Celie fixin' to shave Mister in the movie *The Color Purple*. I could hear the drums and my people crying out in our tribal language. All of this was in my head of course, but the moment called for a little dramatic fun to take the edge off.

My Crown and Glory

I took to the bathroom mirror with my husband's clippers. My mother-in-law and Elajah stood in the doorway watching with eager anticipation of the end result. From the front of my head to the back, I shaved off the remaining locks, taking back pieces of myself with each stroke until the hair was no more. I looked in the mirror at the finished product and saw my eyes big and bright. I saw my smile wide and beautiful. I saw my head -- small but perfectly round. I felt different. A weight had been lifted and I knew that victory was mine. *I still had a crown of glory, even with no hair at all.* I had uncovered my crown of virtue, self-respect, power, and inner beauty, and that could never fall into a sink or be swept away with a broom. I won the battle that day, and with a little makeup and some earrings, my victory looked as cute as can be. It was official; I was a member of the happy, dancing "bald club."

Don't Be a Victim

"A belief is only a thought you continue to think.
A belief is nothing more than a chronic pattern of thought,
and you have the ability -
if you try even a little bit -
to begin a new pattern,
to tell a new story,
to achieve a different vibration,
to change your point of attraction."

~ Abraham-Hicks

When experiencing a disease of any kind, it is easy to feel victimized by a condition that was suddenly introduced into your life and robbed you of your peace of mind or good health. It is normal to feel resentment, anger, insecurity, frustration, and fear when you see changes to your body image. No one wants to look in the mirror, not like what they see, and not be able to do anything about it. That is painful, and yet in order to GROW through the experience, we cannot afford to remain in victim mode.

We have to find our own unique way to fight back and maintain the quality of our lives, Develop a mindset that keeps you sitting in the champion chair with a position of mental strength. Your mind is your most powerful muscle, and even if you cannot change what is going on in your body, you can change your attitude, which will impact your overall experience. It is really just that simple and yet mastering our minds and emotions is not an easy task.

I want you to know that no matter what your issue is, everything you need to overcome it is inside of you right now. You can reassign the value you place on any given situation in your life. It is a skill you can develop through practice with issues big or small. For example, many women who undergo mastectomies as a result of breast cancer understand what it feels like to have a part of your feminine identity taken away. It is a journey to feel whole again when a part of you is missing. By redefining your definition of wholeness and femininity, you can move forward and accept what you no longer have, when you focus on all the things that you do have. In order to survive, we must be willing to let go of old beliefs that no longer serve us and adapt a new attitude to manage our new reality.

I recently went to Disney World with my family and Elajah, who is now ten years old, was afraid -- just as I was -- to go on the Space Mountain rollercoaster. We stood on line in fear, inching up to our inevitable two minutes of doom. I used the *Owning your Power* principle to create a different experience. I started to tell myself and her that I was not afraid. The rollercoaster was safe and this was going to be fun and exhilarating and a wonderful opportunity to soar through the air like a bird with wings. I was going to enjoy it because there was NOTHING to be afraid of. Elajah was not interested in my psychotherapy tactics, so she remained in fear but by the time I got to the front of the line, I was ready for the world. I was screaming like the big dudes that looked like they had a death wish and wanted to ride this rollercoaster until the wheels fell off! It was incredible to be on this ride and sincerely screaming with amusement and letting go of my fear to embrace the moment for the fun time it was created to be. It really works!

That was a simple example, but my point is that we can master our minds for both the big and small things in life. **You do not have to be a victim, you choose to be.** When you have a challenge in life, put this principle into practice and when you realize how powerful you are, your self-esteem will grow by leaps and bounds.

Journal Exercise

Write down three instances in the past where you used your power to shift your perspective and create a new experience. What was it and how did you do it?

Identify three areas in your life where you feel victimized. What is the issue and what story have you been telling yourself? What new thought can you introduce that would rewrite it and shift your experience from being a victim to having victory?

_____

_____

_____

_____

_____

_____

_____

_____

_____

_____

_____

My Crown and Glory

Principle 3:

Tapping the Spirit Within

S

There is a place in you where there is perfect peace.
There is a place in you where nothing is impossible.
There is a place in you where the strength of God abides.

From 'A Course in Miracles'
Foundation for Inner Peace

We are spiritual beings having a human experience, and our purpose here on Earth is to facilitate the evolution of our souls. It is the constant process of coming back to center and releasing the love that wants to be expressed through us. All of mankind is interconnected with nature and God's creations. Men and women were created in the image and likeness of God as co-creators, endowed with the power to take a simple thought and manifest it into a tangible reality. To deny or ignore our innate divinity aborts the blessing of peace, purpose, passion, and prosperity that is available to us. It is not my intention to convince you of which spiritual path or religion to follow, to preach a sermon, or tell you how to live your life. For Principle 3, my objective is to awaken your consciousness to the awareness of the importance of having a spiritual practice in place, and passionately encourage you to tap into the power of the spirit within you with all your heart.

Your spiritual growth plays a pivotal role in your personal development for healing and to build a healthy self-esteem. Knowing **WHO** you are is important, but you cannot move into your full potential in life until you accept and embrace **WHOSE** you are. If you are searching for your identity, please understand that you are first and foremost a child of God and if you did not know, He loves you just the way you are.

There will inevitably be seasons in our lives that will bring more storms than our little umbrellas can handle. Being spiritually grounded allows us to withstand the rain and create a life with relationships that are rich, soul-satisfying, and purposeful. Attuning our ear to hear and be led by our inner voice provides strength and clarity as we journey through the stages of life, until we return to our essence. A spiritual foundation will be the anchor to hold you through the storms and a lighthouse to lead you out of darkness and into safety.

When it Rains….

After about five years of living with alopecia areata, I learned to cope and find serenity by accepting the things I could not change. I wore a wig every day and learned to explore makeup application techniques to make myself look and feel more attractive. I was grateful that I had the option to cover up my head with a wig, and no one would really have to know that I was bald unless I told them. I felt compassion for people who endured changes to their body image in places they could not hide. If wigs were not an option, I would have been forced to go outside bald or keep a hat or scarf on just to avoid the uncomfortable stares from people who lack empathy and etiquette. My wig was my safety net and the only way I felt comfortable being seen in public and even amongst most of my family and friends. It is one thing to have to look at yourself and feel uncomfortable, but combined with the pressure of managing your differences in society, just going to the grocery store causes additional stress. When you can't hide the problem, you have to carry that burden everywhere you go whether you feel up to it or not. Handling the inevitable comments and questions will either make you strong quicker or cause you to revert inward and become less social.

I finally had a mental handle on alopecia, and I chalked it up as a personal challenge I would just have to manage. Everyone has one; alopecia was mine. But one morning I woke up to find a black and blue bruise on my leg. It did not hurt to the touch but it sure looked like it did. I thought back to my activities from the previous day and I was perplexed because I knew that I had not done anything to cause that kind of bruise on my body. "Honey, did you punch me in my sleep?" I joked with my husband.

He smiled, denying the accusations, but sharing equal concern for the sudden bruise discoloring my beautiful brown skin. It was weird, but I felt fine, so I did not think too much of it. The bruise faded away within a few days, but then a new one appeared on my arm immediately afterwards. It was a repeat of the same scenario. By the third bruise, I knew it was an issue I needed to look into. My health generally was good and although I did not have any pain, my body was clearly telling me something was out of balance. I grew increasingly concerned and I was ready to know what it was trying to say.

I visited my primary care physician, who drew my blood right away to check all my numbers. After looking at the results, he expressed concern and told me that I needed to see an oncologist immediately. I did not even know what type of doctor an oncologist was, but I agreed to go. He gave me the address and the nurse made an appointment for me within that same week. On the day of my visit, I put the address in my GPS, but I did not do any prior research about the facility. I pulled up to the address and the sign on the building read "Cancer Treatment Center." I thought I had come to the wrong location. Why would he send me to a cancer treatment center? Unless . . .

In that moment, my mind was racing with fear. I did not know what was about to happen and I could not stop myself from thinking of the worst possible scenarios. *What if they said I had some form of cancer? I am already bald. Isn't that enough?* I wished that I had brought my husband with me for emotional support. Something was telling me that by the time I walked out of this appointment, I would not be the same woman I was walking in. I sensed that I was on the verge of having yet another life changing experience.

I had never been to a cancer treatment center

before and I walked in with obvious apprehension. I was a 31-year-old African American woman, yet the majority of the patients sitting in the waiting room was Caucasian and looked to be over 60 years old. I felt like I did not belong there and, being concerned for what the doctor might say to me, I did not want to be there, which showed in my demeanor. I registered with the nurse at the front desk, who confirmed that I was unfortunately in the right location. As I sat in the waiting room, I said a few silent prayers under my breath. I eventually made a trip to the bathroom because my nerves were becoming frazzled thinking about the possibilities. Within a few minutes, a nurse opened the door and called my name to come in. It felt like Judgment Day and it was my turn to go meet with my Maker.

I followed her through the corridor. As we walked, we passed the room where cancer patients were sitting in chairs, crocheting and reading books while plugged up to

IV machines as they received chemotherapy. My knees buckled a bit as I caught the eye of one old man who was plugged up to the machine as he sat in a chair watching people walk past the door. He looked as surprised to see me as I was surprised to be there. *You have got to be kidding me*, I thought to myself as I followed the nurse quickly back to the room. *If this doctor tells me I have cancer, I am going to pass out and someone is going to have to come and get me because I can't handle this*, I thought.

The doctor came in, charts in hand, and introduced herself. She was a lovely woman, very friendly and personable. After checking for swollen lymph nodes and obvious signs of illness, she ordered additional blood work, which was done on the spot. I sat waiting for the results and when they came back the nurse quickly escorted me into the doctor's office, where she was sitting at her desk ready to discuss her findings.

I sat down and braced myself, relying on my chair to keep me sitting upright just in case her words knocked me out. Fortunately, cancer was not my diagnosis. I breathed a deep sigh of relief, feeling as though I escaped it this time around. No one can predict what life will bring, and no one is exempt from the possibility of being diagnosed with a disease, not even children. I feel such compassion for anyone who does have to experience cancer, and I understand what it feels like to get a disease that changes the course of your life.

My test results indicated the development of additional autoimmune diseases. Twenty-five percent of patients with autoimmune disease will develop additional autoimmune diseases in their lifetime. The name for this condition is **Multiple Autoimmune Syndrome**. Apparently, besides my alopecia areata, I had developed

ITP (Idiopathic Thrombocytopenic Purpura) and **Pernicious Anemia**. Just like alopecia, these diseases were something I had never heard of before, and their names alone intimidated me. The doctor gave me the medical facts in lay terms so I could understand what was going on inside of my body.

She explained that ITP is a blood disorder in which the immune system destroys your blood platelets, which are a component of your blood necessary for normal clotting. My body was destroying my platelets, which caused my platelet numbers to fall dangerously low and the unexplained bruises on my body. Pernicious anemia is a vitamin B12 deficiency. It causes a decrease in red blood cells, which are responsible for carrying oxygen to your entire body. Pernicious anemia occurs when your intestines cannot properly absorb vitamin B12.

On paper I was in a pickle, but thankfully I had felt

fine up until my diagnosis. According to the *American Autoimmune Related Disease Association (AARDA)*, there are over 100 known autoimmune diseases. Medications are available to treat symptoms, but there are no cures and researchers do not know definitively what causes them to occur.

Thankfully, there were medications available that could help treat my conditions. For the Pernicious Ane-mia, my doctor started me on a series of B12 injections to bring my levels to normal. She explained that to stay healthy, I would now have to get B12 injections regularly for the rest of my life. She then went on to discuss the worst case scenarios and potential treatment options for ITP. She suggested that we begin with a prescription for high doses of prednisone steroids, which would hopefully result in an increased platelet count. If none of the medications or procedures available were successful and my platelet count continued to drop, I could experience the sudden and severe loss of blood from my digestive tract, or worse, bleeding into my brain, which is rare, but potentially fatal.

Like I said, I knew I should not have come to the doctor alone that day. I sat there numb with fear as my tears began to fall in disbelief. The doctor gave me time to compose myself and take in the new information. I did not know why I was so unlucky that life would keep giving me challenges I did not feel that I could handle. Losing my hair was one thing, but hearing a doctor say that I could potentially lose my life was a whole new level of sobriety and for a brief moment, the only thing I could feel was sorry for myself.

My thoughts immediately went to my two little daughters. There was no way my husband could handle cooking or doing their hair if I was not there. My poor babies would surely go around looking like some mother-less children. How sad would they be if they did not have a mommy to care for and sing to them, and how depressed would my husband be if he had to raise them alone! I felt a sense of sadness, but deeper than that feeling was my instinct to fight. I had too much to live for and plenty of living I still intended to do. I had heard the facts, but thoughts of dying or being sick could not be entertained. I wasn't about to let ITP or any other group of alphabets suddenly come up and snatch my life after all I had been through. The very thought of it offended me. I got angry, which helped me focus really quickly.

"What do we need to do?" I asked my doctor, wiping away my tears as the conviction to win rose up in me. "I will do whatever it takes." She assured me that we would work together as a team to bring all my numbers back to normal. I trusted her expertise and left feeling optimistic, grateful, and yet sad all at the same time.

My family and friends shared the load of emotions that I brought back with me from the doctor that day. Prayers were being petitioned before God on my behalf and we united our faith that I would be healed and all things would be brought into balance. With proper treatment, consistent follow-up, and the excellent service of my doctor and nurses at the treatment center, I successfully beat ITP. My numbers slowly rose with every visit, and after about a year I was completely off of medication with a stable platelet count. The disease has remained in remission ever since.

That experience was more than just a storm; it was a profound awakening for me that mere words cannot express. Sometimes blue skies can only be fully appreciated after you have spent enough time living under gray clouds.

A Friend in Need

Having a disease of any kind, especially one that could be life threatening, will change your perspective about a lot of things. Suddenly, you don't care to sweat the small stuff anymore. There is no time or energy available to be wasted on foolishness. Every day you feel good above ground is a good day by default. It doesn't matter what is actually taking place, at the end of the day it's all good.

Underneath the physical layers of this experience was an opportunity for spiritual growth that increased my faith and taught me how to lean on and trust God in a brand new way. When a doctor says there is no cure, faith becomes your medicine. *Faith gives you courage and hope for the future knowing that relying on the letters G.O.D. override the knowledge base of a PhD.* There will be moments in life where you will require strength beyond your own capabilities. Grief and illness are some emotions that can be too heavy to carry alone. Fear can be crippling enough to make even the strongest man too physically weak to get out of bed. But there is a force that lives within us and provides a limitless supply of everything we need to move forward, even when our feet seemed to be frozen still.

We see this miracle in action in little children who run around the hospital laughing with joy even when their bodies are ridden with Leukemia. We can see the manifestation of this force through the light in the eyes of people with disabilities who may not be able to formulate words, but still share genuine smiles and love with strangers as they pass by. In spite of their circumstances, they are not bound to a state of bitterness and anger, but they are free to elevate and live on a higher vibration through the expression of love. Relying on our spiritual strength gives us mental stamina to work through the trials of life, by making a conscious decision to surrender the things that are too heavy into the hands of God. We do not have to try to carry a boulder up a hill, for we know that God's yoke is easy, and His burden is light. His grace is all-sufficient, and He bears our sins and grief when we allow Him to be our closest friend in need.

As children of God, we must be reminded that it is our Father's desire that we do not lean so much on our own understanding because things will not always make sense or seem fair. There is only a fraction of our lives that we actually control. Natural disasters, horrible acts of evil, famine, disease, life, and death are all facts of life that teach us that there is a higher authority that we must all yield to. Once we do so, he will direct our path and see us through when the way seems unclear or our hearts have been broken.

Tapping the Spirit Within

Without a spiritual relationship and practice in place, we are more susceptible to becoming self-destructive in our attempt to manage or mask our pain in life. Too many of us fall prey to using drugs, alcohol, sex and every other crutch you can think of to escape our reality. That is a recipe for disaster, and a trick of the Enemy to deter us from the light of God and woo us into a deep sleep of darkness. We can better avoid these temptations by having an effective prayer life and communion with the spirit within.

I would not be who I am today, and I would not have been able to endure a lot of my emotional hardships if I did not have a relationship with God. I openly acknowledge and give Him ALL the praise and glory for everything that He has done for me. He continues to build me up and use even the hurtful situations to be a blessing in my life and the life of others. It is truly amazing to experience firsthand the transformative power of the Holy

Spirit as He performs a miracle in your life, taking something negative and turning it into a positive. That power has been a gift in my life and I wish that for every man and woman on the face of this earth.

If you do not have a spiritual practice in place, you need to create one. Doing so will allow you to develop your faith muscles, experience greater joy in life, and love and accept yourself fully. You will become a better person all around, able to contribute to the healing and unity of the world as your divine assignment. There is no greater self-esteem than to rest in the knowledge of your own divinity. As we must partake of natural food daily to survive and grow, we must also feed our spirit regularly for it to flourish. Fighting through life circumstances will deplete you, so you must consciously invest in your own restoration keeping your cup full and running over as a reservoir for love and strength. Nothing just happens, so be intentional about your spiritual growth. Make it a daily priority, like eating, sleeping, and exercise.

Feeding your spirit should not feel like a chore you have to complete or like a homework assignment you procrastinate in doing. Do what feels good for you. Spending time with God should be as satisfying as enjoying any of your favorite meals or drinking a cold, tall glass of refreshing ice water on a hot summer day. It takes time to discipline yourself to make it a habit, but when you do, it should bring you joy, fill in a place in your heart, and make you feel whole, at peace, connected, and at one with God.

When religion leaves you feeling burdened, weighed down with dogma, rules and traditional rituals that no longer provide spiritual development, that is a sign that you need to re-evaluate your beliefs. It is okay and necessary to be willing to change your mind in search for the truth. God is not concerned with your attendance record in any religious organization, he is only concerned with the condition of your heart and your life. Stay alert so that you do not get complacent by simply following the practice of doing what everyone else is doing. Without a relationship with God that allows you to hear his voice and causes you to grow, everything else is just a form of fashion. Tap into what stirs your spirit and makes you feel alive. Don't be afraid to explore new things. God is not limited to one way, so get out of the box. Like the title of my favorite children's book by Nancy Tillman, God wants you to know, *Wherever You Are, My Love Will Find You.*

Exercise:

Write down at least three things that you can begin to do authentically to move forward on your spiritual path. Here are some ideas for practices you can start to put into place. Use your journal space to document what your barriers may have been, how you plan to move past them, and what you intend to implement and when (you should commit to a date).

A. Attend regular church services at a place of worship that suits your personality and makes you feel inspired and connected. Be willing to visit different places to find one that will be a good fit. Church is not one-size-fits-all. It is a personal fit like any sacred relationship.

B. Attend Bible study to engage with others and share information.

C. Read the Bible and/or other spiritually based books daily.

D. Develop a daily prayer life (If prayer is new to you, simply start by reciting the Lord's Prayer (below) and verbally express gratitude for your blessings. Just start talking to God with faith, knowing that your heart is being heard even if the words escape you.

E. Read and watch spiritually uplifting books/tapes and DVDs.

F. Attend conferences and fellowship with others.

G. Use guided meditation to center yourself and tune in to your inner voice.

H. Listen to music that inspires you and feeds your spirit with encouraging lyrics that build you up.

I. Practice yoga for physical and spiritual strength.

J. Spend time connecting with nature through hiking, long scenic walks, trips to the park, or visits to the beach. Wherever there is peace, God is there.

K. Tap into your creative energy through the arts. Create music, dance, paint, or express yourself in whatever way flows through you freely and brings you into awareness of your oneness with God. Co-create a masterpiece and bless the world with your gifts.

The Lord's Prayer

Our Father, which art in heaven,
Hallowed be thy Name.
Thy Kingdom come.
Thy will be done in earth,
As it is in heaven.
Give us this day our daily bread.
And forgive us our trespasses,
As we forgive them that trespass against us.
And lead us not into temptation,
But deliver us from evil.
For thine is the kingdom,
The power, and the glory,
Forever and ever.
Amen.

Matthew 6:9-13 KJV

My Crown and Glory

_____

_____

_____

_____

_____

_____

_____

_____

_____

_____

_____

_____

_____

_____

_____

_____

My Crown and Glory

Principle 4:

The Practice of Forgiveness

S

"As I walked out the door toward my freedom,
I knew that if I did not leave all the anger,
hatred, and bitterness behind,
I would still be in PRISON."

~Nelson Mandela

One of the emotions that weighs us down and hinders us from experiencing the fullness of peace and joy is *resent-ment*. Holding on to anger, hatred, and bitterness stunts our growth and blocks our blessings. The principle of practicing forgiveness is a crucial component to the healing process. In my opinion it is more difficult to forgive ourselves than it is to forgive others, and both of these are equally important.

We tend to look at forgiveness as something that should be earned and not freely given. We may fear that forgiveness would be perceived as a sign of weakness, or that we will be taken advantage of if we let the person who hurt us "get away with it." In reality, some people who hurt you may not even ask for forgiveness. They may never admit their shortcomings, show remorse, or change their behavior at all, but all of that is irrelevant to the goal you seek to accomplish, which is PEACE. Focusing on that and moving past your pride requires some introspective work. Forgiveness is about regaining personal power. It is a decision we make to untangle ourselves from the past, let go, and set ourselves free. By acknowledging the hurt and the hate, we open the door to new possibilities. This does not mean that we have to reconcile the relationship with the person who offended us, nor does it mean that we excuse the offense. It is simply part of the liberation process that signifies that we are ready to heal, and open our hearts to love again.

The first lesson of forgiveness is to understand that it's NOT about the wrongdoer -- this act of faith is all about YOU! Forgiveness is the most powerful action you can do to align yourself with the flow of blessings in your own life. No one is perfect and one day the forgiveness you give will be the forgiveness you need. There is no way around it. To get to the land of freedom, you MUST walk down the path of forgiveness.

Soul Food

I was happily married and my life was headed in a positive direction. I felt good about me and proud of all the work I had done to finally love myself enough to cultivate the healthy and loving relationship I always wanted. I felt like my past was behind me, until it ran up on me one afternoon while I was walking in my old neighborhood. I was headed to my mom's house for Sunday dinner and some quality mother-daughter time, which I always enjoyed very much. She only lived 15 minutes away from me, so I took advantage of the opportunity to indulge in her homemade soul food when my favorite dishes were on the menu. On that particular Sunday, I made a quick stop at the check cashing place near the candy store.

As I parked my car and locked the door, I saw a familiar face walking down the block. It was my childhood boyfriend. He was my very first heart break and the boy I lost my virginity to. I had not seen him in years and that was just the way I wanted it! He was heading in my direction, and he had the audacity to be looking at me as if he intended to approach me. Our eyes met and I quickly turned my head to avoid his gaze. Shaken and confused, I hurried into the check cashing place. *How dare he even look at me*! I had half a mind to go back outside, run up on him, and slap the taste out of his mouth, just because he had it coming to him for years. The site of him made me so angry that I wanted to retaliate for the years of hurt I suffered because of his actions. I stood in the checkout line wrestling with all of the emotions from the bad memories that flooded my mind at the sight of him.

It all happened when I was in my last year of junior high school and he was a freshman in high school. We were friends from the neighborhood and his best friend went to the same school I did. I liked him because he was witty and smart. He had a great sense of humor and he did not try to act tough like the other boys did. We would sneak calls and spend hours on the phone talking, laughing, and getting to know one another. I enjoyed the attention I got from him and the feeling of closeness I had with him, even though he was a bit shy. When he could, he would meet me after school and walk me home. I was comfortable with him and I considered him a friend.

My parents did not allow me to date at that age, but that did not stop me from having an interest in boys. Living in an apartment building afforded me the privilege of a secret kiss on the staircase every now and again without their knowledge. My parents were clear about their religious beliefs and expectations for me to follow God's plan of waiting until I got married to have sex. They were from the South and very old school, so conversations about sex were taboo in my home. The most my mother would say to me was, "Don't let those little boys fool you." I did not really know what that meant and I dared not ask. She would follow up that directive with, "And you better not let me find out about it," which was intended to put the fear of God in me. It certainly worked; I was fearful. But I was also confused. I had to manage my emotions, my teenage hormones, and the fairytale fantasies I had dreamt up from watching too many Disney movies by myself. Without having an outlet to discuss the feelings I was clearly forbidden to have, I became a sneaky little girl. The kind of girl whose parents have her on lock-down to protect her, so when she gets a taste of freedom she doesn't know what to do with herself. I was angelic in front of my parents and I was an excellent student with no behavioral issues at school. Unbeknownst to my parents and teachers, I was actually headed down the wrong path --and quickly.

My parents both worked full-time jobs, and my older sister went to work directly after school. When I got home from school each day, I would be alone for a few hours until my mom got home from work. I was not allowed to have company in the house when my parents were not home. To keep me from running the street and getting into mischief, I was also not allowed outside during that time. My mom would call the house soon after I got home from school, and I had better pick up the phone to confirm my arrival and that my homework was being done. I knew the routine and I followed suit. I had hard-working, responsible parents that brought me up with good Christian values and morals. I can really appreciate that today, but as a child I felt like I was in jail, and even with the structure that was provided for me, my low self-esteem caused me to slip through the cracks and fall into disobedience. Young girls often look for love and validation in all the wrong places, which can lead to promiscuity. I was not looking for sex, but I thought it was a prerequisite for the love and attention I was searching for.

The secret staircase kisses soon graduated to an invitation for him to come to my house and watch television with me when my parents were at work. I reasoned that just a few minutes alone would not hurt, and my parents would never have to know. We played that game for a while pushing the envelope every time until we became overly confident and comfortable. I knew good and well that if my mom came home and found a boy sitting on her couch -- even if he was reading the Bible and speaking in tongues -- she would whip my butt! She might have whipped his too because he should have known better! I wish I could say I quit while I was ahead, but I had a hard head which made for me a soft behind.

In typical teenage fashion, when given ample space and opportunity the kisses soon turned into heavy petting, which turned into the loss of my virginity. That was an unmemorable, complete waste of five minutes. It was nothing like I thought it would be, and I automatically regretted it, and him. I gave my virginity to him to prove that I loved him, in hope that he would love me in return. Looking back, the act was never about me or my sexual needs. It was a classic emotional struggle many young girls (and even grown women) deal with. Many of us feel pressured to have sex to keep our guy interested and win his affection. We think that if we don't have sex with him after a certain amount of time, he will break up with us and give the love we desire to someone else. One of the biggest mistakes that young girls make is to undervalue themselves. When we don't know our worth, we give ourselves away to an undeserving soul out of peer pressure and an obligation to make them happy.

A Love Note to my young ladies: Losing your virginity is sacred. If it is not saved for the covenant of marriage, it should <u>at least</u> be shared <u>safely</u> with someone you love and with whom you share a mutual commitment. Sex is not a game for child's play. There are a lot of emotions involved and potentially serious issues that can arise, such as STDs and unplanned pregnancies. Your body is your temple. You are valuable and once you give your precious virginity away, you cannot get it back! Choose wisely from your heart, AND use your head.

This experience was a hard enough lesson I had to learn. Unfortunately, the class was just beginning...

The School of Hard Knocks

One day later that week, my boyfriend came over to visit after school as usual, only this time he brought his best friend. I was also friends with this boy, and we had just spent time laughing and joking during lunch at school earlier that day. The three of us sat on the couch talking and watching television, just like we would normally do, but on that day my boyfriend was acting differently toward me. He was normally pretty shy, and had never behaved aggressively before, but suddenly he was sitting close to me, putting his arm around me and trying to kiss me. It was clear to me that he was showing off because his friend was with him. I thought his behavior was obnoxious and I was angry that he wasn't being his normal self. I felt uncomfortable, confused, and disrespected. I did not understand why he felt the need to show off this way.

As his friend sat on the opposite couch watching, he leaned in close to me and whispered in my ear, "Let's go in the bedroom and do it again." He was smiling at me with wide eyes, like a child anticipating a gift on Christmas Day. There was a cocky arrogance about him as he played the part of a ladies man in the one-man show he was putting on for his friend. I looked at him with shock and disbelief. *Did he really just say that to me?* He was sincerely trying to play me for a fool. Did he think I could not see that his only objective was to set me up so his friend could watch? At what point had I become some whore that he could use for entertainment? In exchange for the love I had given to him, I was paid in betrayal, and I was devastated. Feeling dirty and used, I pushed him away, yelling, "Hell, no. Get off of me and cut it out!" His friend laughed at his failed attempt at being smooth and suave. His ego bruised, my boyfriend's countenance immediately changed. The cold look in his eyes let me know that I had crossed over into enemy territory. He was ready to go to war and I felt like a wounded soldier about to be put out of my misery.

"Okay," he said as he stood up, "Since you won't give it to me, you're going to have to give it to both of us." The room grew cold, and I felt as if I had just stepped onto the set of a horror film. His friend took the cue and stood up to join him, almost as if this had been their plan all along. With a threatening look in their eyes, they stared at me like two bank robbers waiting for me to give them money out of the register. Terrified, I stood up and ordered them to leave immediately. My so-called friends who I had known for years were not playing a mean joke; these boys were serious and they intended to prove it.

They both grabbed me and I fought them, yelling profanities as they pulled me into the bedroom. They threw me on the bed. While the friend held my arms above my head, my boyfriend climbed on top of me attempting to undo my clothing. They were both laughing with guilty pleasure as if this ordeal was funny to them. It was clear that if I would just hold still, they were going to have their way with me. Instead, I kicked my legs and screamed at the top of my lungs for them to get off of me, wriggling desperately to get myself out of their trap. I fought so hard, purposely kicking toward my boyfriend's genitals so they would be forced to abort their mission.

I shudder to think of what they would have done to me if I had been scared into submission, too afraid to fight back. They did not have any weapons, so I was willing to fight them both with everything I had. My rage gave me the courage to withstand what turned out to be one of the most horrific moments in my life. I could not decide what felt worst, being betrayed by two so-called friends, or my broken heart. Defeated and frustrated, they finally let me go. I stood up, ready to keep fighting, yelling for them to leave. There were no drugs or alcohol involved, not even a cigarette to blame for their behavior. They were stone-cold sober, so the only thing I could think of was that this was clearly a real-life invasion of the body snatchers!

They continued to rough me up a bit, pushing me up against the wall, mashing me in my head and calling me names. They both stood in front of me, yelling obscenities in my face like drill sergeants, and all I could do was stand there with my arms folded, clothes and hair disheveled, and just take it.

"You're a stupid bitch because you gave it up to me," my boyfriend said. "And you're not even my real girlfriend, Candice is," he said with an evil laugh.

I felt so stupid, and I wished I could make it all disappear. I kept my face together, determined not to give them the satisfaction of seeing me cry.

"Look, my mom will be home soon, you guys have to leave!" I shouted angrily. The boys were not moved, and seeing me get a spanking would be just the perfect ending they were looking for. It would be a great payback for the insult of me not giving them what they wanted. Besides, she could not really do anything to them. She didn't even know who they were.

To prove to me that they were running the show, the boys sat around on the couch flicking through the channels with the remote for a few minutes before they finally decided to leave. As they left, they taunted me at the door, putting their feet in the way so I could not close it. When they had as much fun as they wanted, they finally went out the door and down the elevator, leaving me alone to crumble into a million pieces. I fell to the floor crying and screaming hysterically for the few minutes I could still be by myself. I could not believe what had just happened to me, and that my life had fallen apart in a matter of minutes. *This was my fault*, I thought. I deserved it because I should have listened to my mother. I never should have had a boy in this house. He was right, I was a stupid bitch. I thought he cared about me, but all this time he was only using me to get what he wanted. Why couldn't I see that?

My mom would be coming home soon and I had to have my face clean and eyes white so she would not suspect anything by the time she walked through the door. I could not tell her what had happened to me because I thought she would kill me! (Well, not literally, but close enough.) The last thing I needed was a spanking or a verbal thrashing to finish off the night. I had no more fight in me, so I would have to lean on my skills as an actress to get through this next episode.

As a child, I had acquired the skill of masking my true feelings and pretending to be okay when I really wasn't. Acting offered an escape from the pain in my life by allowing me to constructively channel any negative energy to become someone else for a moment. By the time my mother's key was in the door, all was quiet on the set. As the door closed behind her, it was time for the scene to begin.

"Hi Mommy," I said, sweetly greeting her at the door.

"Hey, what's up," she replied, obviously tired as she took off her coat and hung it in the closet.

"Nothing much, I'm good. How was your day?"

"It was fine," she said as she thumbed through the mail on the table. "How was yours?"

"It was oh . . . kay," I said. I stood there at the dining room table looking at her intently, but she had her head down as she focused on the mail. It was not okay. The tears filled my entire body, and they were pooled up right behind my eyes like a dam waiting to break. I wondered if she sincerely could not see them or if she chose not to. I waited a moment until she looked up at me, then said, "Well, I'm kind of tired and I have a headache. My homework is done, so I'm going to go lay down."

She didn't think anything of it. She had worked hard all day at the post office and was anxious to get in the shower and just relax and have dinner. Inside I wanted to fall into her lap and cry like the baby that I was. I needed so much to be held and consoled, but I could not say a word. I did not break character; I got through the scene and my performance was brilliant. There was no applause, and there were no encores and no awards. My compensation was the tears spilt as I cried to sleep that night and for many nights afterward. All I could think was

"Momma was right; I should have never let those little boys fool me."

Salt in My Wounds

It was just my luck that the dynamic duo felt as though ruining my reputation should be their next order of business. When I went to school the next day, I was bombarded by so-called friends who heard the latest rumor about me losing my virginity to my boyfriend. I was known as "Sandra, the innocent little church girl," so this was some juicy gossip that those kids could not believe. My boyfriend had put my business all out in the street, and it was greeting me at the lunch table and everywhere I went. I was shocked and pissed! Hadn't they done enough? What exactly were those boys trying to get me to do, kill myself? Why did they suddenly hate me so much? I did not know what I could have done to deserve this treatment.

I knew I had let that relationship go too far, and it

had been out of character for me to entertain a boy by letting them come to my house. I did not need anyone else to weigh in on my mistakes, so I fervently denied the rumor, trying to maintain what little self-respect I had left. Good thing I had become such a good actress. I was getting a lot of practice for my high school days as a drama major at the High School for Performing Arts.

I think everyone believed my lie except for the posse of boys that always stood in front of the candy store. They were my boyfriend's friends from the block, and they had heard the gossip, too. I had to pass by that candy store on my way to and from school each day. From that day on, every time I walked by, I heard sniggles and giggles and got stares that sent me taking the scenic route home to avoid them. Sometimes he would be with them and every time he looked at me I felt my stomach drop. I hated him and his friend with a passion. Since we lived in the same neighborhood, I saw him many times after that day, but we never spoke again.

Eventually I stopped crying and moved on with my life. I was still devastated, however, and I always wondered what I could have done to make those boys turn on me the way they did.

My parents never knew about any of what happened. They always did what they could to shelter me from the evil of the world and give me a good life. But maybe I was a little too sheltered because my sense of reality about the world was too pure. I pictured the devil with horns and a pitch fork; I did not know he was a chameleon or maybe I was just a poor judge of character.

Next in Line

It had been nearly 10 years since that incident, but standing there in line at the check cashing place, it all came back to me. After my initial knee jerk response of anger, I settled into the truth of how I felt. I really was over it. It did not hurt anymore. Seeing my ex-boyfriend's face struck a nerve in me, but I had actually forgiven him years before. I had to because the pain was eating me alive. It certainly contributed to the low self-esteem that led me into the abusive relationship that nearly ruined my life. When I made the choice to leave that relationship, I started my healing process by forgiving EVERYONE who ever hurt me whether they knew it or not. I realized that other peoples' dysfunction is NOT my fault and I had to stop blaming myself and taking on that responsibility. This guy missed out on a good thing and whatever his reason was for treating me that way, was not justified. I learned that when it comes down to any form of abuse, people who hurt others are usually those who are hurting themselves.

My ex-boyfriend walked into the check cashing place and came straight to me, clearly intending to break the years of silence. I was caught so much off guard that all I could do was brace myself for what he might say. I had had many conversations with him in my mind over the years. I had narrowed what I would say to him, if I ever got the chance, down to a few choice words. Now, in front of all these people, I was going to stand center stage and deliver my heart-wrenching monologue but he didn't give me the chance. He had a desperate look in his eyes, and when he opened his mouth, it was to rip the band aid off the old wound once and for all. Without even a hello to break the ice, he dove right in.

"I'm sorry," he said. "I am so sorry for what I did to you when we were kids. I want you to know that I did love you! You didn't do anything to deserve that and I am really sorry. You were my queen and I've hated myself knowing that we could have been together all this time. "

I stood there in silence, hearing his heart and watching the sweet young boy I used to talk to on the phone for hours surface right before my eyes. Where the hell had he been all this time?! I had convinced myself that that kid must have been a figment of my imagination.

He went on to explain that he grew up without his mom in the home. He was raised by his dad and older brothers, who were all womanizers. The behavior he showed me was the behavior he had grown up seeing. He had been taught that as a man, that was the way you were supposed to treat a woman. He didn't have any other examples to follow. Yet he knew deep down inside that it was wrong. He was young and wanted to impress his friend, but it went too far.

"When I turned 18," he said, "I knew that I would never be a man until I told you these things. It has bothered me all of these years, and I wondered how what happened must have impacted your life." He went on to say that he saw me now, beautiful and happily married, and he knows that could have been us because he really did love me all along.

Wow. I stood there, overwhelmed with gratitude. He needed me to release him from the past he was still holding on to. He needed my forgiveness as much as I had needed to forgive him way before that day. I had the power and fortunately for him I had already forgiven him and there was nothing but love left to give. We could not change the past, as much as we both might have wanted to. Hearing him actually say the words I always wished he would say, healed me in a hidden part of my heart. He was brave to approach me and apologize without knowing how I would respond to his exposure of such a deep wound. With his words, he took off the bandage and found my scar, but it had already been healed. I was not the one bleeding anymore, he was. I felt his sincerity and I wanted him to experience the peace I had felt, so I simply hugged him. It was the most honest response, given from the bottom of my heart. We stood there in line hugging and I said softly, "I forgive you. It's okay and I'm okay. Yes it hurt and it messed me up for a while because I did not understand why you did that to me. But I understand what you are saying. I got over it and I moved on. I'm really okay now and I am happy."

It was a moment of victory for both of us, and it was a long time coming. The healing power of forgiveness freed us both, and taught me a wonderful lesson. That scenario could have played out in so many ways. I could have lost it and put him in a headlock! I could have missed out on Sunday dinner with my mom and ended up having to get bailed out of jail instead! Not cool. I am grateful that our chance meeting ended with peace and not war. I have not spoken to him again after that day, but I don't have any anger towards him in my heart. I wish him well and I forgive him for the way he treated me and the damage it caused. I am free to move on, leave my past in the past, and create a wonderful future and so is he.

Forgiving someone does not mean that they have to become your Facebook friend or follow you on Twitter. It is okay to love someone from afar and just let that water pass under the bridge. People come into our lives for a reason, a season, or a lifetime. We help each other learn valuable life lessons through the experiences we create. When we learn the lesson, we can move on. The pill of

The Practice of Forgiveness

forgiveness is like a horse pill-sized vitamin that gives you strength when you swallow it. No matter what someone has done to you, forgiving them gives you your power back. The power they may have taken away is replaced with love and peace, even if they never have the courage to apologize. Remember that a life well lived is your best revenge. Instead of focusing on your wounded feelings, learn to look for the love, beauty, and kindness around you.

The Karma of Forgiveness

We must develop and maintain the capacity to forgive.
He who is devoid of the power to forgive, is devoid of the
power to love. There is some good in the worst of us and
some evil in the best of us. When we discover this,
we are less prone to hate our enemies.

~ Martin Luther King, Jr.

"For all have sinned and come short of the glory of God."

Romans 3:23 KJV

This scripture is a sobering truth to meditate upon when

faced with the challenge of forgiving someone. We have

all come short of God's glory at some point or another.

Like me, I am sure there are things that you may have

done wrong to someone that you want to be forgiven for.

It could be big or small, but at the end of the day, no one

is perfect. We all have a past and we are where we are in

our personal development today as a result of our experiences and the choices we have made in our lives.

Ultimately, we must exercise *compassion* for one another because we all want and need the same basic things in life. Whether rich or poor, black or white, male or female, our core essence is the same. We are children of God in need of healing and forgiveness. The pain inflicted upon you could have been premeditated, an ignorant mistake, neglect, or flat out abuse. Whether the person will recognize it, acknowledge it verbally and apologize, or turn away callously with selective amnesia, your peace lies solely in your ability to forgive them anyway. We are not defined by the painful experiences we have, but strengthened through trials to prove that we can take a lickin' and keep on tickin'!

We cannot erase the past or win the war by fighting now against what happened back then. Our emotional wounds are like our fingerprints. They are unique to us, and no one is exempt from getting imprinted. I think of the scars caused by the emotional wounds inflicted on me as tribal marks. I have been initiated into a group of people, warriors who understand pain. We are warriors who have endured the worst of situations, and are still alive to tell about it. We come forth with greater understanding of ourselves. We come forth with deeper compassion for others who experience pain. We come forth as leaders to lead the way and pull others up out of their pain and into the promise of peace that we have come to know. If you really want to experience healthy self-esteem, choose to forgive as you want to be forgiven and you will be one step closer to your freedom.

The Practice of Forgiveness

Exercise

1. The first step of this exercise is to create some quiet time where you can be alone and uninterrupted. Make a list identifying the people you need to forgive, and for what. Be specific. Put yourself on that list too and jot down the reasons why. Take some time to pray and reflect on this issue. There may be people and hurtful experiences that automatically come to the forefront of your mind. Jot those down, but be still and allow those unconscious issues of deep silent resentment to surface. Uncover every secret thing whether it is big or small. You can't run from your pain. It will always be there unless you take this time to purge it. None of those ill feelings will serve your highest good, so don't hold on to them. Surrender it all.

2. Call up the memories one by one to your mind. Allow yourself to feel the pain and emotions that come up for you. Let the cleansing tears flow for all the years they may have been suppressed and ignored. Now is the sacred time. Take deep cleansing breaths and press through this moment until you feel some relief. It won't be a one-shot deal. Forgiveness is a process. You will have to revisit these emotions and work through them until it doesn't hurt anymore. You will know when that happens because you can talk about the issue and not cry or get angry. The sting of it will be gone and you will know that you took your power back and you have truly forgiven that person and/or yourself.

3. Another good thing you can do is talk to that person if it is a healthy situation. Say what you need to say once and for all. Communication is the key and you may be pleasantly surprised. Sometimes we hold on to issues and

experience hurt only to find out later on down the road that we had it all wrong. Things could have been miscommunicated or not communicated at all, leaving you to draw a false conclusion. What if you found out you were wrong about things the whole time? There are always three sides to a story: your side, their side, and the truth. You might sincerely understand the other person's perspective in a brand new way that could melt all the pain away instantly. The problem could be resolved, but you will never know unless you try.

4. If verbal communication is not possible, try writing the person a letter. Depending on the circumstances, you may or may not want to or physically be able to give it to them. The goal is for you to get those feelings out. This person could be living or deceased. If the person is deceased, you could visit their gravesite, read the letter there, and then burn it. This is about moving forward in

freedom, so don't hold on to the past. Let go and let God!

5. Forgiveness is not forgetting. It is not about pretending that the offense did not occur. It is about acknowledging hurt feelings, but deciding to leave them in the past. You don't necessarily have to understand the offender or the offense to forgive it. Do it regardless, simply because forgiveness is essential to have peace. If you are having a difficult time, talk it through with a skilled life coach or therapist. Whether you were hurt intentionally or unintentionally, recognize that it does not serve you not to forgive. It directly impacts your mind, body, and spiritual growth. If you are a parent, the implications of your inability to forgive can be far reaching. Through your words and your actions, you send a clear message to your children about forgiveness. Think about the message you want to send and commit to lead them down the right path as you walk it out before them.

The Practice of Forgiveness

_____

_____

_____

_____

_____

_____

_____

_____

_____

_____

_____

_____

_____

_____

_____

My Crown and Glory

The Practice of Forgiveness

_____

_____

_____

_____

_____

_____

_____

_____

_____

_____

_____

_____

_____

_____

_____

_____

_____

_____

My Crown and Glory

Defining Success

for Yourself

S

"I've come to believe that each of us has a personal
calling that's as unique as a fingerprint -
and that the best way to succeed is to discover what
you love and then find a way to offer it to others in
the form of service, working hard, and also allowing
the energy of the universe to lead you."

~ Oprah Winfrey

For Principle 5, we will take a close look at the definition of success and how your beliefs about it have helped create the life you live. From childhood, we are taught that success is measured by the attainment of high grade point averages, college degrees, money, material things, accolades, and even popularity. Some messages are direct, while others come subliminally from the media and society at large. Some are even perpetuated within our own families. As we move into adulthood, we often find that our life choices were based on what we have been told and not necessarily what we believe to be true. At some point we have to wake up to ourselves and take an introspective assessment of who we are and what we really want out of life. To build healthy self-esteem, you must begin by telling YOUR truth and making a commitment to live it even if that requires you to move in a brand new direction. It is not a group decision; it is a personal one that we all must make. You can let your light shine at the maximum wattage or you can stay frustrated, dimmed by the lampshades of beliefs that you have chosen to live under. Taking off these lampshades can be difficult, but I have found the results to be worth it. Don't waste precious time living in a shadow. You will never manifest the life of your dreams until you learn to embrace your own rhythm and stop marching to the beat of someone else's drum. *Sing YOUR heart's song; it is the divine soundtrack to your life.*

My Crown and Glory

Adulthood is Overrated

To this day, my mom would tell you that I was the kind of child that wanted to grow up fast. I could not wait to be an adult and I would let her know that often. I just wanted to do what I wanted to do and not have to follow anyone's rules. I never considered all of the responsibilities that went along with being an adult, just the freedom part. At 19 years old, I moved out of my parent's house to live with my husband, not too long after we started dating. My parents were not pleased with that decision, especially since "shacking up" was contrary to the values with which they raised me. I was working administratively for the NYC Department of Education full time while attending college part time. I had become a responsible young lady, doing the right things, so I felt mature enough to move into full-fledged adulthood. I did not have a clear vision for my life or specific goals for my future. Looking back, success to me was merely survival. My plan -- outside of becoming a famous R & B Diva, of course -- was to get a good-paying job, work hard, finish school, and figure out the rest as it came. It did not take me a long time after I moved out to realize that being an adult was overrated. I had to manage all of the household bills, cook and clean every day, work full time, manage my homework, and maintain a relationship. I did not have anybody to tell me what to do, but somehow I was still expected to get all those things done. I felt bamboozled: all that hype and I still ended up having to wash dishes every night!

Two years later, we got married, and two and a half years after that, we had our first daughter, Miyah (My-yah). When she was six months old, I started a career at a major telecommunications company. This would al-low me to make more money and give me opportunities for growth and development within the company. I did not have an interest in telecommunications per se, but it was a "good job" with "great benefits" and I was happy that I passed the exam to start in the entry level position of Customer Service Representative.

Soon after initial training was over and real life on the job began, I realized that being chained to a desk and telephone all day was not the ideal work environment for my personality. I felt confined and bored answering the same questions all day long. After a year, I focused my attention on becoming a manager in the call center so I could get out of my seat regularly and explore my innate leadership skills. I was promoted to management, given a healthy raise, and made responsible for a team of 25 customer service representatives in a sales and service environment. I was proud of myself and my family celebrated my success as well. I was moving up the corporate ladder and the sky was the limit for the possibilities of continued growth, status, and income.

> "Learning what does NOT make you happy is just as important as figuring out what does. Clarity can be found in the process of elimination."

~ Sandra Dubose

It did not take me very long to realize that the corporate "needs of the business" were becoming more important than the need for me to leave work on time, to get my daughter from the babysitter, and home for dinner at a decent hour. This new role was all-consuming and began to impact the overall quality of my life. I was stressed by the demand to put in long hours as a salaried employee that ended whenever the job was done. As a new manager, I wanted to prove myself by achieving the goals and sales objectives that were expected of me, but that was predicated upon the performance of my team. I traded in the familiar simple script of general billing questions for the opportunity to be yelled at all day by irate customers instead. I got to experience the not-so-fun games of office politics, favoritism, and managing union representatives that ran the office with a Mafioso air. I learned a lot about leadership and what it looks like, up-close and personal, to be a good leader and a bad leader. I was grateful for the lessons, but I felt out of place. I was losing touch with my true self and taking on a new role of Mrs. Corporate America. I wondered if this was what success looked and felt like. From the outside looking in, I was doing very well in my life. On the inside, I began to experience a turmoil that indicated that I was out of balance and an alignment was inevitable.

Any time you begin to stuff yourself into a box to fit a mold that has been preset by standards you did not create and cannot control, you will become uncomfortable and eventually unhappy. Our work life should be an extension of ourselves that allows us to contribute to the success of a company in a way that feeds us, not one that drains us of our energy. Many people believe that having a job or career that we actually enjoy doing is a luxury set aside for a select group of "lucky people." Out of fear, we settle for the security of what is familiar even if it is unpleasant or does not meet our needs. When choosing a career path, the first objective is to know your skill sets, strengths, and personality traits. Then seek out a position that allows you to be authentic without having to shrink or deny the best part of who you are. If you don't, those concessions will begin to eat away at you and infect other areas of your life whether you realize it or not. Too many of us die a slow death, hidden behind job titles that have become work prisons, and slowly, but surely, the glimmer in our eyes begins to fade. We live for the weekends or our two-week vacations, when we can breathe again and become alive for a spell, only to get depressed when the time comes to go back to our prison cells. The classic rat race pervades our society, leaving many disgruntled people with heavy hearts and shattered dreams.

Unraveling

I worked for five years in that management role before the walls of truth came tumbling down. At that time, my alopecia experience had begun to spiral downward into complete hair loss and I was devastated. My confidence was shot and I was insecure in my marriage. I felt like my body was talking to me and screaming for relief from the stress I had lived under for the past several years.

By that time, I had given birth to my second daughter Elajah (E-lay-jah). She was a beautiful handful of love, but a colicky baby that stayed up late at night crying when we needed to get up early in the morning. My life was not going in the direction I wanted it to. It felt like a runaway train and I wanted to get off and take a different path in search of my happy place. In the meantime, I would sit miserably anticipating that glorious day when I could jump off that train. I was not happy within myself, therefore, I was unable to experience joy in other areas of my life. My marriage was a source of frustration, my job was draining me, my hair was falling out, I felt ugly, and I did not even enjoy being a mother to my two daughters. Life was overwhelming and they became just another chore to manage throughout my busy day. I was impatient with them, often angry, and emotionally unavailable. On most days, I did not want to play or laugh or tickle any children. I just wanted them to eat, bathe, be quiet, and go to sleep so I could have some time of solitude to cry and pray for divine guidance.

My family and friends knew that I was unhappy in my role as a manager. I searched for a new position within the company, but there was nothing available at the time that I qualified for. I would have to wait indefinitely until something else opened up, but time was not on my side. I knew that I needed help ASAP because I was slipping into a depression. I had been there and done that before, so I knew the signs all too well. I started to see a therapist for the first time in my life. It helped to have his ear as an objective sounding board even if he did just nod and listen every week. I had knots in my stomach every morning I got up to go to work. I wanted to call out sick daily and wished I would come down with some non-life-threatening illness to give me just cause to stay home. It got to the point where I would sit outside the office crying in my car unable to go inside for an hour each morning. I could not fix my face to pretend that all things were well and the thought of talking to an irate customer scared me. I was so angry inside that I could snap and retaliate at any given moment. Something had to give because my strength was giving out.

I told my husband and family that I wanted to

resign and find a new job that made more sense for me and actually made me happy. I was an artist and as a creative person I knew I had more to offer than brainstorming ideas of how to increase sales to meet caller ID objectives. I did not care about caller IDs, and I felt like I would jump out of my skin if I had to keep talking about them! The responses varied from person to person, but the consensus from my inner circle was the same: they all seemed to think I should stay. "You make great money there. Are you really willing to give that up?" "The benefits are awesome and you're not going to find another job that will pay you that kind of money." "If you know what I know, you better hold on to that job whether you like it or not." "I don't like my job either, but you do what you have to do." "You need to focus on your children and think about their future." "You can be happy after work hours; you get paid to do a job." "You have too much debt to leave; you better stay and just ask God to give you strength." "These feelings will go away and you will be okay eventually."

I began to understand that everyone has their own path in life and each of us, whether young or old, are doing our very best to find our own way. *To expect others who are fearful and have limited beliefs for their own life to speak freedom into yours is an unrealistic expectation.* People cannot give you something they do not have. When you want to get advice, seek counsel not only from the people who love you, but from those who are living a life that exemplifies the life you actually want to live. Ask them how they achieved their goals. Do not take advice from someone who has the same problems that you do. Even with the best intentions, your loved ones can keep you locked in a state of fear that will dim the vision that you have for your life. Everyone may not see the vision you have for yourself or share the same high expectations for life. They may not cosign on the sacrifices you may be willing to make in order to give birth to the person you want to become. Don't wait around collecting votes on your destiny in order to please a majority. Your path is a personal choice and the people who truly love you will support you whether they agree or disagree. Learn how to step out on faith, to hear and trust the intuitive voice of God within you. Only there will you find the courage to do the things that everyone else said cannot be done!

Shaking Free

One morning I started on my way to work, going through the usual routine of dropping my children off to school and the babysitter. My emotions were weighing especially heavy on me this particular day, but I managed to go through the motions of getting myself together and off to work.

It had become the norm for me to sit in my car in the parking lot of my job, working the knots out of my stomach and praying tearfully for enough strength to get me through another day. That morning I needed a word of encouragement, so I called my best friend, Sala, on my cell phone. Through all of the voices that weighed in with more concern for my pocketbook than my overall well being, hers was the voice that heard my heart's cry. We had been friends since our freshman year of high school and she knew I had talent and skills that would never be fully utilized or appreciated in a stuffy corporate environment. There was more to me, and Sala would speak life to remind me of who I really was and the possibilities that lay just beyond my fear. She would say, "God is bigger than that job and He is not limited to just that company. You don't have to stay anywhere and be miserable; a door will open up for you that will make sense." She was the breath of fresh air that gave me just enough hope to pick my face up off the floor and get out of the car.

I thought I was okay after my morning pep talk with Sala. I headed inside, walking slowly past my team of representatives, avoiding their eyes and giving a weak salutation to the entire group. I sat in my cubicle at my desk facing my computer. I felt numb all over and I could not focus my mind on anything. My intention was to check my emails and pull the morning sales reports, but in actuality I was sitting there staring at my computer and it was staring blankly right back at me. I was in a dream-like state where my mind and body moved in slow motion. One of the customer service representatives decided to jump start my day by calling me over to her desk to take over an irate phone call. "This customer wants to talk to a manager, Sandra!" she exclaimed. I had overheard the conversation because the representative sat right outside my cubicle. I understood why the customer had become aggravated and the call had escalated. The representative's tone was unpleasant and rude as usual. It was obvious that she really did not want to do her job, but neither did I that day.

I got up slowly and sat at her desk to review the account. I have no idea what the customer wanted, but whatever it was, I gave it to them. I let them rant and rave, then I apologized profusely like a programmed robot and offered a solution that provided outstanding service and made the customer happy. I handed the phone back to her to complete the transaction and she became angry that I did whatever the customer asked me to do instead of backing her up. She wanted to be right and prove the customer wrong. I wasn't taking sides, I wanted peace and I became infuriated with her for disrupting the little bit I had with her ego.

On the walk back to my desk, I suddenly became overcome with grief. A wave of emotions was rising up on me and I could feel my eyes filling up with uncontrollable tears again. I could not breathe and right there in the middle of the call center I felt like I was about to have a nervous breakdown. I made a bee line for the elevator just to avoid the crowd. I made it inside just in time before my knees buckled. Crying hysterically, I ran outside to the parking lot and called Sala again. "I can't do this Sala, I'm losing it today," I cried. "Sandra, enough is enough," she said. "Get out of there! Nothing is worth all of this. This is killing you. Why are you doing this to yourself? It is not healthy and it is not going to get any better. You need to leave." I realized that she was right. I was clearly running on empty. Nothing in my life made sense anymore and I knew deep inside that God would provide, but I was going to have to trust Him enough to get out of the safety box I created. I needed some time to breathe and decide what was best for me. If this was success, I did not want it and no amount of money was worth the price of my peace of mind and happiness. I would rather work for less money in return for more joy. It was clearly a sacrifice I was ready and willing to make, and I did not need anyone's approval anymore to do what was best for me.

"I want you to fix your face, go back upstairs to get your pocket book, tell them you are going home sick today and then leave. Call me when you get back in your car and you are finally on your way home." Salas instructions were clear, and clearly my only option. My nerves were frazzled and I was not any good to anyone in that state. There was no way I could even fake being productive on that day. I would surely embarrass myself if I stayed any longer and risked exposing my wounds for the entertainment of others.

I did as instructed. I fixed my face, and like a zombie I went back upstairs and headed quickly to my desk. I did not stop to talk to anyone for they would clearly see that I had been crying. Standing there at my desk, I grabbed a bag and started to fill it with everything of mine that had any sentimental value. I took the pictures of my family, my notebook, my favorite pen, inspirational quotes posted on my cubicle wall, and a few items of company paraphernalia I had collected over the years. I turned off my computer and whispered a final good bye to my things. I had made a handful of friends at that job, but I could not stop to say goodbye to them. I just had to go. I walked slowly, seemingly in slow motion toward the door looking peacefully at the familiar faces I had worked with for the past six years. Everyone seemed to be engaged in caring for customers on the line. They did not notice my quiet departure. I had to tell another manager that I would be leaving, so I went to my trusted friend and peer to give her the message to deliver. She was alone in her office and she noticed the look on my face as soon as I walked in the door. "Hey baby girl, what's the matter with you?" she said lovingly as she always had.

"I am not feeling well, Valerie, I need to go home today," I responded. My eyes told the entire story and she knew I had been going through some changes lately.

"Sure, do what you have to do. Are you okay?"

she asked with sincere concern.

"Not really, and I don't know when I will be back. I just know I have to go. I can't do this anymore," I confided. We both welled up with tears. She could feel my pain and she hugged me like the big sister she had always been to me.

"Don't you worry about anything," she said. "I will let the other managers know and we will work it out. You just take care of yourself, okay?"

I loved her for not making me feel guilty or like I needed to explain. She simply released me with love and I felt free, but sad at the same time. This was not the way I ever wanted to leave, but I had waited too long. My cup became too full and the bottom had fallen out. All I could do was take one step at a time and begin the process of restoration to adjust the dial of my life until I found a channel for peace.

I got in my car and called Sala right away. "I did it, Sala," I cried. "I left and I am in my car on my way home," I screamed with a voice of freedom.

"Yay, Sandra! Good for you, girl. You did the right thing. How do you feel?" she asked as she cried tears of joy with me. "I feel free and happy and scared, but much better. You know my husband is going to kill me, right?" We both laughed in agreement, but I knew that even if he was initially angry, he would ultimately understand.

My husband always supported my decisions and had my back whether I was right or wrong. I could count on him for that, and he did not disappoint me. The money concerned him, but not more than my health and sanity. I would take some time off and work on finding a new job. This wasn't the end of the world; it was just the beginning of a new life for me. If it meant I would be better and a happier person, I didn't see how anyone who truly loved me could argue with that and I was right.

On the drive home, I prayed and thanked God for the strength to stand up for myself and my truth. I knew that I was being swallowed up in that experience, and there was something more that He had for me to do in my life. There was an environment somewhere that would not only be conducive to my health, but it would be a place where I could grow, flourish, and fully pour my heart into. I wanted to reconnect with the free-spirited, happy, creative woman I used to know before I buried her underneath a pile of spreadsheets and sales reports. I needed to laugh heartily and sing out loud again to hear my own voice. I had a song aching in me that I needed to release or I would surely die. I had become a shell of a mom, missing out on my children, and I hated myself for not giving them the fullness of love I know they deserved. Driving down the highway, I released tears of joy and gratitude. I was grateful for the spirit of courage to jump out of the box and finally say yes to the universe. I felt the familiar feeling of being shaken free and awakened out of a state of apathy. My mind began to race with ideas and excitement about the life I could create with a clean slate. I let go of my worries of what everyone else was going to say or think about my decision. All that mattered was figuring out what was next for me. Who did I want to be? What was my new vision for my life? I had the power to call the shots, and now I was awake and ready to do it. Life was no longer going to just happen to me. I was ready to set my intention and purposely position myself in a place where I could be all-the-way me!

My first desire in that moment was to go and pick up my daughters. Miyah was four and Elajah was just one year old. I felt light and joyful when I saw their little faces. I picked them up and hugged them for a long time. In my heart, I was apologizing for being missing in action for so long. I was making a silent covenant with them to always be fully present and not miss out on another opportunity to give them all of me. They were too young to understand, but I know they felt the difference and saw a new sparkle in their mommy's eyes. I took them to the park and for the first time, I simply watched them play. They were no longer a chore; they were my source of joy. Miyah pushed Elajah on the swing and I sat on the bench watching my children as if I was seeing them for the first time. I heard their laughter and it was a beautiful sound. I had told them to be quiet for so long, I lost appreciation for the sound of true happiness that comes from the innocence of a child. I felt so blessed to be awake and I knew that no matter what sacrifices laid ahead monetarily, in that moment loving my children the way I did, I had all the riches I needed.

Good Success

> "But as it is written, Eye hath not seen, nor ear heard, neither have entered into the heart of man, the things which God hath prepared for them that love him."
> **1 Corinthians 2:9 KJV**

I love to tell this story because I know that so many people can relate to how I felt on many different levels. It was a pivotal turning point in my life when I made the choice to hear, trust, and honor my own voice at any cost. As a result, my life has continued to unfold in the most miraculous ways, and I have never had one moment of regret. My sick leave led right into a convenient layoff the company was experiencing and subsequently offered a buyout package to managers like me to leave with pay. My good friend, Valerie, called to give me the good news, and it felt like Christmas Day. I now had both the time and the finances I needed to figure out my next move without worries. I was in my happy place, and I never had to step foot back in that call center again. Every need was met and then some. It was a wonderful testimony of God's amazing grace that is always in sufficient supply. I was proud that I mustered up the faith to step off the cliff into the unknown, and learned that not only could I fly, but the wind would carry me up to heights I never dreamed of.

The road was not smooth or easy, but neither was my job at the call center. It was the right choice for me and a huge step in the direction I needed to go to readjust my life and bring it into alignment with my core values. The voice inside of me that no one understood or could hear was for my ears only. It was a sacred secret and promise for an abundant life, available to me only if I trusted God enough to commit to use my talent and gifts to be a blessing to the world. This book is just one example of that divine secret being revealed through His perfect wisdom and timing.

For many people the layers of others' expectations are so deep. Our desires can become buried underneath them as we try so hard to make everyone else happy. The little muffled sound of our inner voice can get drowned out by the sound of all of the voices in our ears. I used the scenario of my work experience to illustrate this principle, but it applies across the board. Consider some of these other examples of how things can play out in life when we do not commit to live our truth:

- Many students go to college and get a degree in majors that they have no interest in simply to please their parent/guardian or just to acquire a big paycheck. The result is a disgruntled college graduate headed down a career path that they do not want to be on. Sometimes that revelation comes a little too late and they find themselves back in school taking out additional loans to study the subject they are actually interested in.

The lesson: Listen to your heart the first time and exercise some faith that your passion will lead to profit and your divine purpose.

- Some people lose their footing because they are trying to follow in someone else's footsteps or live in their shadow. Having a positive role model is one thing, but ignoring your path to walk on someone else's is another.

The Lesson: You miss out on living your best life when you focus on being a carbon copy of somebody else. That will never bring you true happiness even if everyone else is applauding your efforts. At all costs, to thine own self be true.

- In some families, there may be cultural traditions or religious beliefs that keep us going in circles instead of moving forward into greater realizations of ourselves. I know firsthand how difficult it is to break away from family beliefs for fear of rejection and disappointment. All of those consequences are possible, but your conviction to live your own truth has to be strong enough for you to withstand the potential backlash. When one person stands up and lives their truth, their light shines bright and illuminates the darkness for everyone. Everyone is not ready to walk in the light and the glow may anger them by hurting their comfortable eyes but don't apologize for your glow. It is not your job to keep everyone comfortable at the expense of the quality of your life. Those who truly love you will want you to be happy and eventually accept your decisions.

The Lesson: Stand up for what you know to be true for you and take ownership of your own life. You might have been born and raised within a specific belief system, but sometimes as adults we change our minds. It is okay and natural for us to outgrow circumstances or people. Decide for yourself which path authentically meets your needs and facilitates your growth. The evolution of our souls is the ultimate goal not the pacification of others.

Exercise

1. Create some quiet time to get still and tune in to your inner voice. Ask yourself the hard questions and journal your answers. How do YOU define success? Don't think about what you have been told. What does true happiness look like for you?

If you are not achieving the level of success you desire, ask yourself: are you willing to do the work and make the necessary sacrifices? It will take courage. *The word courage is from the Latin word "cor" meaning 'heart.' And the original definition was to tell the story of who you are with your whole heart.* Have the courage to ask for what you really want from your heart.

2. Think about the areas in your life where you are not living your truth. Make a numbered list of them and beside them document the changes you would like to see happen. Commit to move forward in truth in each of those areas. Create some new short-term and long-term goals. If it is a job that drains you, start by identifying what kind of career you would like to have. What steps do you need to take to make that a reality? (i.e. finish school, take an instructional class, volunteer to gain experience, etc.)

If it is your personal life, identify what would bring you greater personal satisfaction (i.e. spend more time with your children or significant other, take a family vacation, go back to church or find a new church). Think it through, make a plan, and begin to execute it step by step. Celebrate every success. Every step completed deserves a pat on the back.

3. Create a vision board. This is a fun exercise that will really get your creative juices flowing and expand your mind about the possibilities. Get a poster board and decorate it with pictures of the things you want to acquire or achieve in your life. Anything goes! There are no rules. It doesn't have to be realistic or immediately attainable. It is a dream that you wish to bring to life, so stretch your mind and don't worry about HOW it is going to happen. That is irrelevant. Your goal is to tell the truth about what you would really WANT to happen. There is no time limit and there are no expiration dates. Don't be afraid to cut out that picture of a Hawaiian vacation and post it on your board. Your dream car and dream home are all mandatory funzies to include in that vision, so go all out. The prerequisite to achieving anything great and manifesting miracles in your life is the ability to see it and believe it. Stretch your faith! If you step out with courage and follow

the plan God has for your life, I promise you that the items on your board will be nothing compared to the amazing blessings that he has in store for you!

Defining Success for Yourself

My Crown and Glory

The Attitude of Gratitude

S

The miracle of gratitude is that it shifts your perception
to such an extent that it changes the world you see.

~ Dr. Robert Holden

One way to manage painful experiences is to focus on the positives. You can find a silver lining behind every cloud if you shift your position and look at things from a new perspective. Counting your blessings will always fill your heart with gratitude, while tallying up the negatives will only make you feel worse. This is a classic example of the law of attraction, whereby you create more of what you want in your life by placing your attention and feelings into manifesting your desired outcome. We are so powerful that we can conjure up negative energy and circumstances when we are consumed by negative thoughts. We have to be conscious of our thoughts, knowing that we are always creating our lives even when we don't intend to. Nothing happens by chance; some experiences are created as a result of a self-fulfilling prophecy. It takes practice to maintain an attitude of gratitude, which we will look at in Principle 6. Even through the most difficult losses, hidden treasures can be found and you will come out victorious with invaluable wisdom gained.

Daddy's Girl

My father, John Dubose, was one of the sweetest people I have ever known. He was born and raised on a farm in South Carolina and moved to New York City when he became a young adult. Growing up poor with his fair share of difficulties in life made him an easygoing and humble country boy. As a result of his meager upbringing, he worked very hard to create a comfortable life for his wife and children. I was always proud to say that he was my daddy because everybody liked him. He was well-known and respected in our neighborhood. As a child, I remember feeling such pride because my schoolteachers adored him. If his work schedule allowed, he would volunteer and chaperone my school trips. While he sat talking with the teachers on the bus, all the kids would ask me, "Is that your daddy?" "Yes" I would smile with joy and say, "Yes, that that is *my* Daddy."

When I was in elementary school, my father would drive by the school playground on occasion during recess, just to check in on me while he was out running errands. He would watch me play for a while before getting my attention by honking the horn of his blue Chevrolet. All my friends would run over to the fence. They were always just as happy and surprised to see him as I was. If we were lucky, he would give us the coins in his pocket to go buy ourselves a treat from the candy truck. His presence always brought a smile to my face and like most little girls, I dreamt of marrying a man one day just like my daddy.

My father stood about 5 feet 9 inches tall with a medium build and a smooth milk chocolate complexion.

My Crown and Glory

His face was clean-shaven except for a neatly combed and trimmed mustache. My dad never left the house without a splash of cologne and his short, soft afro combed neatly into place. My dad never wore jeans or sneakers, and did not even own a pair of either. Even though he was a blue- collar worker, he dressed as if he had somewhere important to go every day. He wore dress slacks, a white undershirt and a perfectly-ironed button-down shirt, which was always tucked neatly into his pants. On his feet were hard black or brown lace-up shoes that required weekly polishing to keep them shiny. Sometimes he would let me help him polish them. I would take that red wooden hard- bristle brush and go back and forth across the top of those shoes until they shined like new. Polishing my dad's shoes was one of my favorite pastimes as a child just to spend time with him. It gave me a feeling of pride to see him with his shiny shoes on.

The Attitude of Gratitude

I will never forget the sound of his signature hearty laugh, which was as infectious as his personality and sense of humor. Although he did not excel in his formal education, my dad was very intelligent, articulate and witty. He loved big words and enjoyed teaching me new ones to add color to my vocabulary.

My Dad was a God-fearing family man who never cursed and rarely raised his voice. He was slow to anger and always behaved like a gentleman, holding doors open for strangers and helping those in need when he could.

My father was an avid coffee drinker. His coffee was always perfectly flavored with milk and sugar and served in a cup and saucer. My fondest childhood memories are of the two of us just sitting together at the dining room table, as he drank his coffee, cracking jokes and laughing. I remember that as far back as 6 years old I would sit there and beg him for a sip. I would talk his ear off about nothing until he broke down and gave me some.

"You're not old enough to drink coffee" he would say with a smile. "It will put hair on your chest."

"I don't care," I replied, intent on having some of the warm deliciousness he enjoyed so much. With a twinkle in his eye he would pour a little from his cup into the saucer and slide it over to me. With no regard for his silly warnings, I would sip the coffee from his saucer like a little kitten lapping up milk from a bowl. He was be so tickled to watch me enjoy it with a big- girl sense of accomplishment. It was a little thing that meant the world to me and it was our special time together that I always looked forward to.

Teenage Drama

I was very close to my dad until my teenage years, when everything began to shift. As I got older, I began to disconnect from my parents. There were a number of reasons for this, but the main reason was that I had disconnected from myself. My sister, who was six years my senior, was the type of child who did as she was told and did not rock the boat. She never gave my parents any real trouble and therefore did not do a good job at making a path for me to run amok. I felt like my parents expected me to be as perfect as she was, but in their eyes I was a wild child compared to her. "Why can't you be more like your sister?" was my mom's regular refrain, erupting whenever I felt the need to push the envelope and challenge her authority. My mom was ill-prepared and ill-equipped to handle a teenage social butterfly and creative free spirit who needed to express herself at any cost. Eventually "Because I said so" and threats of punishment soon were not enough to keep me in the box I felt I was in. The Aries warrior in me was on fire with unresolved pain, anger, resentment and low self-esteem. That, coupled with raging hormones, was a dangerous combination for a rebellious 16 year old.

I know that my teenage years were a very difficult time for my parents emotionally. And, just as I was coming out of them, my father was diagnosed with the auto immune disease **Systemic Lupus Erythematosus, or SLE.** SLE causes the body's own immune system to attack healthy tissues. Symptoms vary from person to person, but it generally can cause inflammation in the skin, joints, kidneys, brain, and other organs. We did not have a lot of information about Lupus at the time, and the doctors were challenged because 90 % of people with Lupus are women. Managing the unknown is the scariest part of dealing with any disease, because you never know what to expect.

Some Lupus treatments can have awful side effects, and life for my once jovial, light hearted father became very painful in every way. In spite of his illness, he continued to work every day. The joint pain in his hands may have slowed him down but he did not let it stop him from maintaining his quality of life. He was motivated by his personal mission to complete the retirement home he and my mom were building on the family property back in South Carolina. They planned to move there once he retired from his job with the Long Island Railroad.

Over time I could see that he was slowing down, and the ulcers on his back– a common Lupus symptom-- made him so uncomfortable that he suffered many a sleepless night. It hurts to see someone you love living with pain when there is absolutely nothing you can do about it. I felt helpless and somewhat responsible because I knew the stress I caused only aggravated him further. That was not my intention, but that did not change the facts or make the situation any better.

One summer day in July of 1994, my mother and I went on a bus ride for a church outing to Hershey Park with my godmother's church. My dad was feeling under the weather, so he stayed home from work and spent the day in bed. My mother thought she should stay home to keep him company, but he insisted that she go without him. He said he would be okay and just needed some rest. We hesitated, but we did believe that plenty of rest would be just the thing to get him back on his feet. We got home late from the park that night and I dropped my mother off outside of her apartment building and drove home. Soon after I arrived, I got a call from my mom. She said that my dad had become increasingly sick through the day and was feeling really bad. He had a fever but refused to go to the hospital. She was in a panic so my boyfriend (now husband) and I went back over there to convince Dad to get help. He reluctantly allowed us to call an ambulance, and they came right away to take him to the nearest hospital.

After admitting him they found that he had pneumonia, but they assured us that he would be fine. They started him on medication right away and we were hopeful that he would come back home in just a few days.

My mom went to visit him the next morning and he was already showing signs of improvement to his normal self joking with the nurses and turning on that charm that seemed to make everyone fall in love with him. I had a temporary part-time job at an electronic store that summer, and after my shift ended that day I picked up my mom so we could pay another visit to Dad in the hospital that evening.

Say What You Need to Say

My mom and I were so happy as we traveled to the hospital. She told me how much it scared her to see him get so sick. We knew that Lupus had the potential to be fatal, but that that was the exception and not the rule. And although it was definitely taking a toll on him, he had only been living with Lupus for four years.

My parents had so many exciting plans for their future once they owned their time and did not have to punch a clock for work anymore. Once they retired, they planned to settle into their home in South Carolina and do some traveling, just like they had always wanted to do. One of their biggest dreams was to catch a flight and finally visit a Caribbean island. As long as my father could stay healthy, they were going to live it up after all their years of hard work.

My Crown and Glory

Mom and I walked into the hospital and stopped to get visitor's passes. We stepped off the elevator on the 4th floor and headed towards Dad's room, giving a wave hello to the nurse's at the station as we walked by. It was a normal day of business as usual and everything seemed peaceful and in order on that floor. Dad was not in the ICU or any special unit. He had a regular room all to himself with no need for monitors or funky tubes to aid in his recovery. He was starting to feel better already and they said he would be going home soon.

When we got to his room door, I walked in first. I immediately caught my father's eye. He had a strange look on his face and his eyes were wild and wide open. He was looking directly at us as if he had been waiting on us and had something important to say, but he could not utter a word. After a few seconds it finally registered to our brains that he must be having an attack of some sort, because he was startled and speechless. By the time we got to his bedside he had stopped breathing. He lay still with his eyes still open. I stood frozen with shock and all my words disappeared in my mouth. My mom jolted me out of my stupor when she screamed, "Sandra, get the doctors. Hurry up!" Her voice was like a gunshot. I took off running back to the nurse's station screaming "Help my Daddy, somebody please help my Daddy!" The team sprang out of their seats, ran into the room and immediately started working on him. They put a tube down his throat, yelling out code numbers I could not make sense of as they performed a series of procedures to bring him back to us. They ushered Mom and I out of the room and closed the door. For a moment, standing outside his closed room door and peering inside the glass, I became hysterical. Just like in the movies, the scene was playing out before me frame by frame in slow motion. I was standing up, but I felt unconscious.

A nurse grabbed me by my arms, looked me in my eyes and brought me back into the present moment. She said to me softly, "Look at your mom. She needs you. Go take care of her." My mom was standing in the corridor, devastated, with her forehead pressed up against the wall as though it was the only thing holding her up. Though the doctors still worked frantically to save him, in her mind her beloved husband of 26 years had just died. In the blink of an eye she became a widow and all their plans for retired bliss were now just a faded dream. The love story was over.

I went to her and took her by the hand. We sat down and I knelt down before her and put my head in her lap like a child. With tears in my eyes, I said," Mommy let's pray together. Let's pray right now that God will save him." This is what I had been taught all of my life. I learned as a child that God can perform miracles, and I remembered the story of Jesus raising Lazarus from the dead. Surely he could help my Daddy if we believed hard enough. I begged God to save him. I would give anything, and do anything, if God would perform this one miracle for us. I looked to her for support but she would not oblige. She just looked at me calmly with love in her sad eyes. She held my face in her hands gently and said, "I already prayed baby. He's gone now."

It was settled for her, but not for me. God had already prepared her for things I did not know. The doctors successfully resuscitated him but he was not out of the woods. They brought him into the Intensive Care Unit. We had just enough time to call my sister, her husband

and my boyfriend to meet us at the hospital. We all sat in the waiting room in silence and confusion, waiting to hear an update from the doctors. When the doctor walked into our waiting room, I could tell immediately what he was going to say from the apologetic look on his face. I could not bear to hear those words come out of his mouth. To avoid the blow, I covered my ears and ran out of the room and down the hallway in shock and disbelief. Eventually I ran out of hallway, and there was no place else to go. I needed more hallways and I needed more time.

I wasn't ready for this. There was so much that I still needed to say. I was only 20 years old and I had never experienced the death of someone so close to me. Losing a parent is supposed to be something reserved for when we're older, and I did not feel like I could handle it. My heart was throbbing painfully in my chest but there was no relief. My mind raced with thoughts of my future without him in it. Who would walk me down the aisle when the time came for me to get married? What about my future children? They will never get to meet him. My adult life was just getting started and he was going to miss out on the good parts. This was just so unfair!

Regret creates an extra painful grief experience. If I had any idea that the last time I saw my father alive would be the last time I would ever speak to him, I would have said all I needed to say. I would have apologized again for all the pain and tears I had caused during those teenage years when he was disappointed in me. I would assure him that I was going to figure things out and make something out of my life one day that would really make him proud. I would have thanked him for never giving up on me--even when I gave up on myself, and for not trying to fight my battles for me, but exercising faith knowing that I would pick myself up and find my way back to love, which I did. I wanted to thank him for advising me to be the kind of woman my mother is, because she is a true example of a virtuous woman that has it together. He was absolutely right and I could see that now. Lastly, I would have told him that I forgave him. For all the things I felt he could have done better and for not protecting me from dangers he never even knew I faced. I harbored a silent resentment towards him but I know that he would have, if he could have.

My father was and will forever be the sparkle in my eyes. I never got to say any of those words because death came suddenly and without apology. I know in my heart that he knows my truth. Even now, 18 years later, I still feel his presence, and I keep his legacy alive with my daughters. My dad taught me many things during our time together, but for this last life lesson on the value of time and how precious life is, I am eternally grateful.

The Attitude of Gratitude

"The worst thing about dying is not living first."

~TD Jakes

The reality of death can be cold and leave a bitter taste in your mouth. Getting past the initial moment of grief was one thing, but moving forward without him was another. My family and I were given his belongings that night at the hospital, after he was pronounced dead and we said our goodbyes. We walked out in a daze, as if we just got knocked out in a boxing match. Our knees were wobbly, and we tried not to look obvious to the outside world that we were hemorrhaging from broken hearts. My family and I walked to our cars in silence, not knowing what we were supposed to do next. We would meet up at my mom's house to start that conversation and make phone calls to inform our family members. Unfortunately, none of us really felt like talking.

My Crown and Glory

I remember watching strangers outside the hospital as they walked by. They were laughing, joking and talking amongst themselves. They were eating French fries and driving cars--going about their business as if they did not notice that the sky had fallen. Didn't they know that my father just passed away?! I became angry and offended. How dare they just go on with life as if his life was not important? I wanted to tell them so they could stop what they were doing and show some damn respect! In my mind I was yelling, *Everybody stop smiling! There is no laughing allowed! Nothing is funny and I want you all to shut up!* How was that possible that they were so unaffected? How could life just move on?

I carried my father's belongings in my hand. He wasn't coming home and he would never use them again. They said he would be okay but they did not know. It was true that he would be going home soon . . . just not the way we planned it.

Live it Up

That moment in my life changed me forever. It crystallized the sobering reality that tomorrow or even the next minute is not promised to anyone, so we can't waist time sweating the small stuff. We get distracted by focusing **too much** energy on trivial things like having the perfect body image, acquiring status, wealth and love relationships. When we measure it up against what matters most, we often see how superficial it is and really not that important when it comes down to life and death. When major life changes occur, we gain greater clarity about what matters most in our lives. Being there to witness my father take his last breath made all of my senses come alive. Beyond the pain and sorrow was the beautiful gift of an awakening and the birth of a deep conviction to live my life every day as if it were my last.

Don't wait for the day when everything in your life lines up perfectly to be happy. That day may never come. The best of times often come mixed in with the worst of times, and moments of absolute perfection are few and far between. *The essence of perfection and the key to having peace lies in your perception and decision to be grateful and happy in spite of your challenges.*

Life is truly about learning how to dance in the rain as opposed to waiting for the storms to pass. Some of us will have to dance through storms so rough, that when compared to other people, it will make their storm seem like a simple rain shower with a rainbow. *Don't spend time counting anyone else's raindrops; perfect your rain dance. And even when your boogie turns into a sad, side-to-side two step, just keep moving your feet and live it up!*

Final Exercise

1. Start a gratitude journal. At the end of each day write down five things you are grateful for, whether big or small. Train your eyes to see silver linings, even within the darkest clouds. Make a conscious effort to focus on the positive.

2. Spend some time thinking about all the things you would love to do in your lifetime. Make a bucket list and begin to incorporate those things into your life, starting now. Set a date for your special adventures and watch your life turn from mundane into an exciting journey.

3. "Pay it forward" by always repaying kindness done to you by helping others. Giving back is the best gift you can give yourself to create a life that is rich, meaningful and blessed.

Name at least five things you are grateful for today.

_____

_____

_____

_____

_____

_____

_____

_____

_____

_____

_____

_____

_____

_____

List some action items for your bucket list.

_____

_____

_____

_____

_____

_____

_____

_____

_____

_____

_____

_____

_____

_____

_____

_____

What are some things you can do to

"pay it forward" in kindness to others.

_____

_____

_____

_____

_____

_____

_____

_____

_____

_____

_____

_____

_____

_____

Epilogue

On March 26, 2011, I competed bald in a local beauty pageant. I made history when I was crowned 2011 Mrs. Black North Carolina USA. It was the only pageant I have ever competed in. I was introduced to the idea by Anthony O. Vann, the Executive Director of Noire Productions, which is the pageant organization that I proudly represent. Initially, when he suggested that I enter the competition, I thought the idea was flattering but silly. I did not see myself as a "beauty queen" and I began to mentally tally up all the reasons why I was not good enough to compete. I was not tall enough, thin enough, pretty enough, young enough and let's not forget about the fact that I was bald! I was not going to put myself out there to be some charity case. I counted myself out before I gave it any consideration.

He challenged my thought process because he saw something in me that I did not see in myself at the time. He reminded me of all the great attributes I possessed, and those attributes were everything his pageant organization represented. He helped me realize that I was already a queen, leading others and inspiring women through the work I did by advocating for alopecia awareness, and sharing my gifts as a motivational speaker and singer. By having the courage to compete, I would help other women embrace their own unique beauty with or without hair. So, becoming a beauty pageant contestant became a divine assignment. I had to search my soul to find my truth and challenge every negative thought that made me feel unworthy of a crown and sash.

I reluctantly took on this personal challenge and jumped out of my comfort zone to do something I had

Epilogue

never done before. It was the catalyst that helped me continue healing my own self esteem, by stepping out boldly proclaiming to the whole world, that I was more than enough. Losing my hair did not take away the essence of who I am. My femininity, my beauty and my sensuality are all still intact just as much as any woman with a head full of hair. I had to believe that for myself, before I could authentically represent that to the world. Competing in the pageant helped me to jump over the last hurdle of self doubt.

Winning the pageant was simply the result of competing well, but my personal victory was won the first moment I walked across the stage and heard my husband and children cheering me on. I wanted my daughters to see me step up to the plate and stand up for what I believe in. I needed to leave a deep well of memories in their mind for them to draw from when life brings them battles they will have to fight. No matter what the judges thought of me, my greatest reward was all that I had come to know about myself just by accepting the challenge. I had taken every hurtful, horrible experience in my life and channeled that pain into power. For every tear I cried and trauma that chipped away at my self esteem, I had slayed the dragon in that one moment with two words......I AM. I knew that I represented a multitude of women who have been hurt like me, and were looking to me, to open up the door to freedom and lead the way for them to enter.

When I won the crown, it was hands down one of the most exciting moments in my life. Every little girl wants to be a princess and the inner child in me was redeemed and given a crown in exchange for her shame. There was no way I could have anticipated all of the blessings that were waiting for me on the other side of that mountain. Standing there in my crown and sash with flowers in my hand, I knew that My Crown and Glory was NOT about my hair. The crown I wore on my head was the reward for enduring the struggles throughout my life. It signified that I was victorious over every device of the enemy that tried to steal my joy and silence my heart song. **I wrote this book because I knew no one could fully appreciate the glory, until they knew my story!** All the glory goes to God because it was his strength that kept me and the light of his love that illuminates my path to this day.

You too have a crown and glory and it has nothing to do with any of your physical attributes. It can never be compromised because it is the essence of your authentic self. It is your virtue, your character and your innate divinity as a child of God. I pray this book will help you to heal so you can see yourself clearly and embrace your inner royalty. *You don't have to compete in a pageant or wear a crown and sash to feel like a King or a Queen. All you have to do is believe that you already are, walk with your head up high and know your worth.* You are an invaluable gift to this world endowed with the power to change your life and become anything you want to be. The sooner you wake up to that truth, the sooner you can begin to create the life of your dreams. Wake up my sleeping beauties; the world awaits you.

With Love- For Love,

SANDRA DUBOSE

Suggested Website Resources:

American Autoimmune Related Disease Association
     www.AARDA.org

NC Alopecia Support Group
     www.AlopeciaCommunity.org

Lupus Foundation of America
     www.LUPUS.org

American Cancer Society
     www.CANCER.org

NC Breast Cancer Patient Support
     www.PrettyInPinkFoundation.org

Rape, Abuse and Incest National Network
     www.RAINN.org

National Domestic Violence Hotline
     www.NDVH.org

National Teen Dating Abuse Hotline
     www.LoveIsRespect.org

National Institute of Mental Health
     www.NIMH.NIH.gov

National Suicide Prevention Lifeline
     www.SuicidePreventionLifeline.org

Life Tribute and Grief Counseling
     www.HonorYourLovedOne.com

About the Author

Sandra Dubose-Gibson made history when she was crowned 2011 Mrs. Black North Carolina, USA. She became the 1st Bald Beauty Queen of North Carolina and brought awareness throughout the state to Alopecia Areata, the autoimmune disease that left her bald starting at the age of 25. She is the Owner and President of Dubose Entertainment and the Alopecia Community of the Triangle. As an Empowerment Specialist, Sandra teaches women of all ages how to experience personal liberation by healing emotional wounds and building healthy self esteem. She is a dynamic, sort after national motivational speaker, radio personality and independent recording artist. Born and raised in the Bronx, Sandra now resides in Raleigh, North Carolina with her husband of 17 years and their two daughters, Miyah and Elajah.

Invite Sandra to speak at your next event!

Learn more at www.SandraDubose.com

Making her independent filmmaker debut, in this documentary Sandra Dubose shares her experience of going bald at the age of 25 as a result of Alopecia Areata, an autoimmune disease.

Featured with her in this film are the lovely ladies of the Link Sister Circle, and in a candid conversation they uncover the origin of beauty and explore the relationship women have to their hair. Prepare to be inspired as you witness Sandra's bravery when she went out in public bald for very first time and did a bald glamour photo shoot to celebrate her liberation.

It's an exciting display of courage and strength that will fill you with tears of joy and empower you to look in your mirror and love the person you see inside and out!

A Dubose Entertainment Production
Produced and Directed by Sandra Dubose
Videograpghy by Rick Mitchell
www.VideosByDesign.com

AVAILABLE AT
amazon.com

243

24028925R00138

Made in the USA
Charleston, SC
12 November 2013